PRAISE FOR

THE DAY THAT CHANGED FOREVER

Dr. Roehl has again reached into the heart of Scripture to capture the essence of its story. From the story of Annas through all the tender works uttered by the Savior from the cross, Tim brings out the full experience through a writer's eye and a pastor's heart. I was moved and blessed as I read this book. Tim brings out the passion of the story and the depth of what God wants us to experience.

Pastor David A. Barner
The Evangelical Church of Oskaloosa
Oskaloosa, Iowa

Dr. Timothy Roehl offers all who seek to know more of Jesus Christ a delightful banquet composed of individual passion-week perspectives. Each serving contains years of scholarly study as well as insights from traveling the Holy Land and are seasoned with Tim's Spirit-filled imagination. Take a seat and enjoy!

Pastor Keith Dickerson
Hope Community Evangelical Church
Lake Oswego, Oregon

In a world full of Jesus books that have passed me by, Tim's story captivated my imagination, taught me intricacies I've somehow missed, and helped me find the Jesus I want to know.

Hugh Halter
Author, *The Tangible Kingdom*

Tim Roehl has been deeply influenced by the Gospel preaching of my father, Dr. Peter Marshall. Especially gifted by God to bring alive the scenes of the New Testament, he made Jesus so real to his listeners that "we could almost hear the rustling of his robes as he passed by," as one put it. In a similar way, *The Day That Changed Forever* plunges the reader into the events of the most dramatic story ever told—the death of Jesus Christ on the cross of Calvary.

Dr. Peter Marshall
Peter Marshall Ministries

In *The Day That Changed Forever*, Tim pulls your foot off the accelerator and provides a way for your head and heart to walk together through life-changing landscape around the cross. His genius is not in the prescription of new insight, but rather in the reflective depth of introducing us to old friends. If you are willing to listen to the fabric of life beneath the surface, the life-changing experiences Tim writes of will mark you in extraordinary ways.

Gary Mayes
Vice President, Church Resource Ministries

Tim is a master story teller. *The Day That Changed Forever* helps us experience the events surrounding the crucifixion of Jesus through the eyes and hearts of those who were there. The familiar story comes to life in a new and profound way for seekers, believers and scholars alike. I highly recommend it for your devotional reading!

Dr. Steve Ogne
Coauthor, *TransforMissional Coaching*

Tim Roehl takes us inside the story of Jesus so we can feel it, smell it, taste it, handle it. The author leads us into a face-to-face encounter. Beyond hearing about Jesus, he guides us toward the opportunity to meet the master in a personal way that will allow us to say, "I know this man!" Standing with the characters at the foot of the cross, Roehl offers us a life-changing encounter.

Robert L. Wise, Ph.D.
Author, *The Son Rises*

THE DAY THAT CHANGED FOREVER

Twenty-One Life-Changing Experiences at the Cross

TIM ROEHL

Regal

From Gospel Light
Ventura, California, U.S.A.

Published by Regal
From Gospel Light
Ventura, California, U.S.A.
www.regalbooks.com
Printed in the U.S.A.

Library of Congress Cataloging-in-Publication Data
Roehl, Tim.
The day that changed forever : twenty-one life-changing experiences
at the cross / Tim Roehl.
p. cm.
ISBN 978-0-8307-4803-7 (trade paper)
1. Conversion—Biblical teaching. 2. Bible. N.T.—Biography.
3. Jesus Christ—Crucifixion. I. Title.
BS2545.C59R64 2009
248.2'4—dc22
2009027678

1 2 3 4 5 6 7 8 9 10 / 15 14 13 12 11 10 09

Rights for publishing this book outside the U.S.A. or in non-English languages are
administered by Gospel Light Worldwide, an international not-for-profit ministry.
For additional information, please visit www.glww.org, email info@glww.org, or write to
Gospel Light Worldwide, 1957 Eastman Avenue, Ventura, CA 93003, U.S.A.

To my wife, Shirley,
my love and completer on this adventure God's given us!
I love you.

CONTENTS

ACKNOWLEDGMENTS

A book is never written in isolation. The Lord always assembles a team to bring to life something He plants in an author's heart so it becomes the reality of printed pages. I'm so grateful for the team He assembled to help me write this book so people can better see and know Jesus! My deep thanks to . . .

My parents, Giles and Phyllis Roehl, who first modeled God's love to me and made sure we not only went to church on Sunday but sought to live our faith the rest of the week. I'm especially grateful to my mom, who has encouraged me to write since I was little.

Marlene Dursheuer, my quiet, dignified English teacher at Sleepy Eye High School, who first encouraged me to try speech competition and introduced me to the writings of Peter Marshall.

Peter Marshall, whose writings helped me "see" Jesus in a life-changing way . . . and his wife, Catherine, who made sure his sermons became books like *Mr. Jones, Meet the Master* and *John Doe, Disciple*. Peter's been in heaven for over 60 years, but his writings still bring heaven to my soul.

The pastors, preachers and friends over the years at Bethel Camp, where Jesus saved me and called me into ministry. You made Jesus real to me!

The people of the two churches that Shirley and I pastored—Grace Chapel in Milwaukee, Wisconsin, and ChristLife Evangelical in Blaine, Minnesota—where many of these chapters first came to life at the beginning of messages. It was a joy to be your pastor . . . to help you know Jesus and to learn about Jesus from you!

The team at Regal, including Steven Lawson and Kim Bangs, who so graciously guided me through the publishing process . . . thank God for people with gifts like yours!

My family—my wife, Shirley, and daughters, Aubrey and Elise, who encouraged my writing journey and gave me space to write when something was coming to the surface of my mind and heart.

Thank you, all—I was the writer, but you made up the team so it could actually happen.

Across the years I have met some "spiritual heroes" of mine, men and women of outstanding gifts and influence, through whose lives Christ has truly changed the world. One of these was Tom Allan of Scotland.

In his early years, Tom had become an agnostic, turned off by what he saw as the powerlessness of the church he had attended as a boy. During the Second World War, Tom was assigned to Allied Intelligence in Europe. One Sunday, with nothing better to do, he decided to accept a chaplain's invitation to attend a chapel service.

That morning, an African-American sergeant sang the spiritual, "Were You There, When They Crucified My Lord?" Tom was gripped by the song, and even more by the reality of the cross.

"I felt that morning that I was there at the crucifixion," Tom told me when I met him, "and that changed my life forever."

It also changed the lives of thousands through Tom Allan's ministry. He became a well-known inner city pastor in Glasgow, a national leader in Scotland, a powerful evangelist in Europe and North America, a close friend of Billy Graham's, and the chairman of Billy's All Scotland Crusade. Although he died quite young due to a heart attack, in the span of his years the message of the cross that he preached and lived transformed many.

When I read Tim Roehl's book, I thought, *I hope many will read this and discover how the Christ of the cross and the resurrection can change their lives, as he did with Tom Allan and so many across the centuries.* What each generation needs is not only a retelling of the story of the cross but also a re-happening of the encounter with Jesus, which happened to those around the cross 20 centuries ago.

Some of the ancient Church fathers would tell their disciples to use their imagination as they read the Bible—to read the story and then imagine that they were there, part of the story. Tim Roehl has used his imagination to do just that. Always seeking to be true to the story recorded in the Gospels, he pictures for us what it might have been like for those who lived through the dark days of Jesus'

arrest and crucifixion and then emerged into the light of his resurrected life through the Holy Spirit.

I thank Tim for helping us to be there, as Tom Allan was, "at the
cross." And my prayer is that many who read will say with full faith
and hearts:

Christ came for me!
Christ died for me!
Christ has risen for me!
Hallelujah!

Leighton Ford
President, Leighton Ford Ministries
Charlotte, North Carolina

HE CHANGED FOREVER

Faces and places may change, but the cast of characters stays the same.

Those words have been true across generations and nations regardless of context and culture. In some views of history, the drama of the human condition is played out in unchanging, repetitious cycles, which bring no hope for the human condition. In that scenario, the universal longings of every human heart are lifted by the promise of higher spiritual evolution by greater human exertion and then dashed by the harsh reality of the corruption of selfish human nature. From generation to generation, we declare, "Those who do not learn from history are doomed to repeat it," and yet, in spite of increasingly advanced education and technology, we still repeat our failures because we can't change our nature.

Faces and places have changed; the cast of characters has stayed the same, and history has repeated itself in every generation and nation . . . until *He* stepped into history and turned it into His Story.

Failure could now be changed with forgiveness.

Destruction could now be changed with restoration.

Division could now be changed with reconciliation.

When Jesus stepped into history, He changed everything . . . He changed history from frustrating cycles to divinely fulfilled culmination. He changed humanity's forever, because He alone can change us from the inside out. He alone can transform our very natures so that they resemble His.

Jesus is the central character who changes the entire trajectory of humanity's history.

I know that He can change the course of a person's life. He changed mine.

I grew up in a churchgoing family. I'm grateful for parents who made it a priority for us to regularly worship together. My earliest understanding of Jesus began with our family prayers. At our meals, we would pray together, "Come, Lord Jesus, be our Guest, let these gifts to us be blessed, Amen." It was encouraging to know that God liked to sit and eat with us. At night my mom or dad would tuck us in and we'd pray, "Now I lay me down to sleep. I pray the Lord my soul to keep. If I should die before I wake, I pray the Lord my soul to take." I never really understood the full import of those words, but it was also comforting that the Lord was with me through the dark hours of night.

Sunday School teachers taught me Bible stories Sunday after Sunday at my home church in Sleepy Eye, Minnesota (yes, I'm a *Little House on the Prairie* kid, having grown up only 25 miles from Walnut Grove, made famous by Laura Ingalls Wilder). The little Sunday School "Pix" comics we took home from class helped bring Bible stories to life in pictures, introducing the stories of long ago into my world. My bathrobe and a kitchen towel became a shepherd's outfit for Christmas programs. I learned Bible verses for Sunday School and Vacation Bible School. At VBS we drank green Kool-Aid, ate cookies and painted plaster figurines for a homemade nativity set. I recently found some of them in a box at my parent's home and I was amazed by the deep feelings those little pieces of plaster stirred up in me.

So, like most kids who grew up going to church like I did, I knew *about* Jesus, but I didn't really *know* Jesus. My faith was more rote knowledge in my head than a real relationship with Him in my heart.

One life-changing night at a summer camp, Jesus came into my heart. I was in the midst of many people who had a quality to their lives that I didn't have. I was a good religious kid—outwardly good but inwardly not even close. I saw something in them that made me yearn to be clean and whole on the inside where no one but God and I could see. I wanted the joy, peace, spiritual familiarity and intimacy in prayer they had. Their inner emptiness had been filled to over-flowing by the fullness of His presence. There was a longing in my heart for this fullness that I had never realized before.

At an evening service on a beautiful, warm Minnesota summer night there at Bethel Camp, I was in the midst of hundreds of people . . . and then suddenly it was just Jesus and me. A stirring message, passionate singing, the Spirit's beckoning and a simple, "You need to pray" from my camp girlfriend . . . and then I was sitting with my head bowed, asking Jesus to come into my heart, to forgive me and make me His own. My plain words from a humble heart were instantly met by the King of heaven's supernatural response. It felt like a cool, cleansing, life-giving stream of water flowing through my insides. A weight was lifted off my heart . . . and I was free! My eternity, destiny and trajectory were forever changed that night. Jesus moved into my heart and invited me to the greatest adventure that human life has to offer. That place in a camp tabernacle among the cornfields, on the western edge of Minnesota, became sacred ground for me.

Thirty years later, while driving with my dad and uncle, we found ourselves near the old camp now turned into a hunting lodge. I asked them to give me a few minutes as I drove onto the grounds (so much smaller than I remembered as a youth). The old tabernacle building looked shabby and uninviting. I went inside and saw there were no pews, pulpit or any other sign that this had been a place where people met God. But when I went to stand on the spot where Jesus saved me, I was overwhelmed with tears of grateful joy. For a few moments, all I could do was stand on that sacred ground, weeping my thanks to my Savior for changing me from the inside out. It became sacred ground again as I looked up with hands raised and tears streaming down my face and whispered, "I'm still Yours . . . I'm all Yours . . ." A relationship that had begun decades ago was just as real now, but deeper, sweeter, purer and even more wonder-filled.

When I came home from camp those many years ago, I *knew* Jesus, but I had an insatiable desire to know *about* Jesus. The Bible beckoned me to learn more about His heart and His promises. I wanted to know what it meant for Jesus to become part of my daily life . . . for Him to understand and care about my struggles and dreams. I wanted more than the Sunday School Jesus I had grown up with. I wanted to know the real Jesus!

In God's providential way, He made sure that a gracious, quiet English teacher in my high school asked me if I wanted to try out for speech. Being a kid from a small town school where you could be a part of just about everything, I said, "Sure, why not?" She invited me to read a book called *Mr. Jones, Meet the Master* by Peter Marshall. I'd never heard of him before, and I found that I was reading sermons written 40 years earlier. At first the thought of doing portions of sermons for high school speech didn't appeal to me, and I told my teacher so. She just smiled at me and asked me to read the book and see what I thought.

Peter Marshall's stories re-created scenes from Scripture with "sanctified imagination," and when I read them, a whole new world opened up to me. Suddenly, I wasn't reading a Bible story about Jesus; I was *in* the Bible story *with* Jesus! Peter made those stories come alive. Jesus strode off the pages of Scripture into my reality. I could *see* history become His Story and blend into my story! I found myself identifying with those who met Jesus in the Gospels and realized that often their story was also my story. I found myself irresistibly drawn to Jesus as Peter Marshall described Him—strong, robust, tender, loving, courageous, wise, generous, gracious . . . supernaturally natural! I found myself saying, "That's the Jesus I want to know."

Peter Marshall's ministry on paper stimulated God's call to me in spirit. God's invitation to help others come to know Him as Savior and Lord became my call and life's adventure. Helping people "see" and know Jesus has been a passion ever since, and it's only grown stronger over time.

As I began to listen to other people's spiritual viewpoints, I came to realize that there are many ways that people look at and respond to Jesus of Nazareth. I often find that people mold the Son of God into an image of their own choosing . . . and often, their own convenience.

Some like a Jesus that's gentle, mild, never offensive, always comforting. He's always forgiving, never judging and will ultimately let everyone into heaven in the end. The alternative is too much for them to consider . . . too uncomfortable.

Others want a Jesus who responds to their every whim with power and prosperity. They use His promises as demands and commands for Him to perform at their bidding.

Still others use Him to justify their own political ends, morphing Him into the standard-bearer for their political philosophy and strategy, using Him as permission to justify whatever means they use to gain power.

Some see Him as otherworldly, and almost wooden—always with a faraway look in His eyes, speaking spiritual proverbs in a reverent monotone but remaining emotionally disconnected from our real world of pain.

Some want Him to only be a wise teacher or good moral example—someone to be admired but not really worshiped in total allegiance.

Others deliberately cut out portions of His story, allowing Him to be a prophet, but denying His death and resurrection that declare Him to be God.

You can probably add more incomplete and even invalid views of Jesus, which highlights the essential truth that how people "see" Jesus deeply affects the way they relate to Jesus.

It really does matter how you see Jesus!

Peter Marshall instilled in me an aspiration to see and know the real Jesus, grounded in how He is revealed in the Bible, especially through the eyes of those who saw Him first. Knowing the context of their world helps me understand the implications of knowing Jesus in my world. I determined that I would blend solid historical research, good biblical language study and what Peter called "sanctified imagination" into retelling the stories of Scripture in a way that would relate to and intersect our stories today.

It's especially important when we follow the stories that lead us to the cross that we "see" Jesus as He is revealed in Scripture through the eyes of those who were actually there. Unfortunately, all too often, the drama and depth of Jesus' journey to and His experience on the cross has been diluted into a more acceptable retelling that doesn't overly offend our senses. Others have removed real people's experiences from the equation and instead focused only on the doctrines that can be derived from the narrative. Others imprint their own image of Jesus on the crucifixion, instilling their agenda instead of Scripture's.

The stories in *The Day That Changed Forever* started as sections of sermons—I sought to help the people I pastored "see" Jesus in a way that was true to Scripture and also timely for their own lives. In illustrating and retelling the stories straight from Scripture, I was also inviting people to relationship with Him.

The cast of characters in the original Lenten drama are so compelling and so contemporary. Peter . . . Andrew . . . Annas . . . Pilate . . . a Centurion . . . Judas . . . John . . . Mary . . . Barabbas . . . Nicodemus . . . the unseen forces of heaven and hell . . . Mary Magdalene . . . two condemned thieves on either side of Jesus. When we enter their stories, we so often see our own.

Most of all, look at the Central Character. When we see Jesus through the eyes of those who were actually there with Him, we can better see Him actually here with us.

Yes, faces and places may change, but the cast of characters stays the same.

Yet there is one Character who stands out above all others. He's the One who changes everything, everywhere, for everyone.

He's the One that changed forever.

He changed my forever.

As you read these stories, my prayer is that you will "see" and know Him, and that He will change your forever, too.

ON THE WAY TO THE CROSS

1

Majesty on the Mountain

(The Transfiguration)

Matthew 17:1; Mark 9:1; Luke 9:28

Before you experience majesty on a mountaintop, sometimes you have to endure misery in the valley.

It started as one of those teachable moments the disciples had come to both anticipate and appreciate. They had been ministering in the area of Caesarea Philippi, a village in northern Galilee renowned for its picturesque setting and its places of worship . . . worship of darkness. A beautiful village at the base of the largest mountain in the region, it was well watered by streams and pools, and green with plant life and trees. But temples to spiritual forces of darkness and to powerful Roman rulers had made those with spiritual discernment sometimes shudder at the oppressive shadows behind the visible beauty. During the days when they were in the region, there were moments when Jesus seemed to be aware of things going on beyond the disciples' awareness, and His face hardened at times with an intensity they had only seen when He was confronting demonic forces.

One day as they walked along, Jesus' mood was unusually pensive. As they stopped in the evening around a campfire, He had a faraway look in His eyes as if He were seeing ahead to things in the future. Looking up at the circle of men who had followed Him for almost three years, He asked, "Who do people say that I am?" From around the circle came the responses: "Some say that you are John the Baptist come back to life . . . others say that you are Elijah—he never died, you know, riding off in a chariot of fire—and some call you one of the many prophets who say they speak for God." The myths and misrepresentations about Jesus throughout the region were many. When His disciples fell silent, Jesus looked at them thoughtfully and said, "But what about *you*? You've been with me all this time . . . who do you say I am?"

Peter, who often found himself the spokesman of the group because of his impulsive way of blurting out whatever came to his mind, spoke this time with a conviction that came from truth that had been forming in his heart for a long time: "You are the Christ . . . the Messiah!" Instant assent from around the circle of disciples echoed his words.

Messiah—for the Jews, this was the one person they had been longing for throughout their history. He would be a man, but more than a man—someone specially sent by God Almighty to come set His people free—supernaturally liberating them from the oppression of slavery they had endured for so much of their journey. Few times since the Exodus out of Egypt, led by Moses, had they seen a leader-liberator who'd been larger than life—so anointed by God that all could see and follow. Yet none of them had fulfilled the prophetic declarations of the prophets concerning the Anointed One. If Jesus were the Messiah, then His inner circle would rise to positions of power, prestige and authority. *That* thought had not been lost on Peter or the rest of the Twelve.

Somehow Jesus knew what they were thinking. He always did. He had a way of looking at people—more a way of looking *into* people, past the external appearance where they normally made their judgments to the heart where the true character and motives resided. He had once taught them that the outside didn't matter . . . it was what came from the heart that made all the difference.

He was doing that now, knowing that their response to the revelation of His true identity was being distorted by their own desire for power. His gaze briefly held each disciple's eye—and heart—before He spoke again.

"You are right in calling me the Messiah, but wrong in what you think I've come to do. I will set people free—not just our own nation, but also all peoples—by setting them free in their hearts. When the heart is free, then families, communities and entire nations can be truly free. Remember that I once told you, if the Son sets you free, you will be free indeed. But the way to freedom will not come as you think. Rather than welcome me, our religious leaders will reject me, torture me and put me to death. But three days after that, I will rise again. It is then you will see the full extent of my work as Messiah." With that He got up and walked away from the firelight, leaving them in stunned silence.

His words shocked them like getting punched in the stomach. Rejected? Tortured? Put to death? And what in the world did He mean by "rising from the dead"? The thought of their Master, who left lives miraculously changed wherever He went . . . who overcame disease, natural disaster, demons and even death itself, with supernatural ease . . . His being defeated by *anything* shocked and stunned them.

Peter got up and followed Jesus into the shadows. This time he spoke in his naturally impulsive fashion, loud enough so that all the other disciples could hear. A thought popped into his mind, and taking Jesus by the sleeve with both hands, he spoke in the way a friend tries to talk to another friend who is speaking irrationally. "But, Master! You are the Messiah! These things could never happen to you . . . nothing is too hard for you . . . surely you must be mistaken!" The other disciples looked bewildered, wavering between believing Jesus' revelation and agreeing with Peter's reasoning.

This time the look on Jesus' face was angry, and his voice was sharp. "Peter, you don't know what you're talking about! Get away from me, Satan! You're only looking at this from a human point of view, not God's!"

The words stung Peter to the core. This time Peter was so shocked by Jesus' words that he had nothing to say. Jesus had been disappointed with him before, had scolded him before, but never had He spoke with such stern authority, rebuking Peter as He would an enemy.

Nothing more was said that night; but Peter lay awake, looking into the darkness long after the others were asleep.

The next day, Jesus was teaching a large crowd, and what He had to say stung Peter again. It seemed that His eyes lingered on Peter before He turned to speak to the audience hanging on His every word.

"Anyone who intends to come with me has to let me lead. You're not the one who is in charge . . . I am. Don't run from suffering . . . embrace it! Follow me, and I'll show you how. It comes from denying your own right to rule your life,

dying to yourself and following me wherever that may lead. If you try to stay in control, you'll lose your life. But if you give me control of your life, you'll save it. What good does it do you to run your own life, get everything you want and lose your soul—your real self that lasts forever—in the end? What could you ever trade for your soul? If you're embarrassed over me and the way I'm leading you, when you get around your fickle and unfocused friends, know that you'll be an even greater embarrassment to the Son of Man when He arrives in all the splendor of God, His Father, with an army of holy angels."

Peter sat listening with his head down, Jesus' words running right through him, laying him wide open, exposing his divided loyalties. Jesus paused and spoke again, this time His voice taking a softer tone. "Let Me say this as clearly as I can . . . some of you here will see it happen—see the kingdom of God arrive in full force." The tone in Jesus' voice made Peter look up at his Master, and he saw Jesus looking at him with tenderness and invitation.

Jesus continued to teach and touch people's lives as He had for almost three years, but the disciples could tell Jesus seemed to be carrying an increasingly heavy load. Instinctively they wanted to reach out to help Him, but none of them knew what to say.

One morning, when about a week had passed, Jesus asked Peter, James and John to come with Him. Without mentioning where they were going, He led them out of the city into the foothills that led up the slopes of Mount Hermon.

Mount Hermon was the tallest point in the entire region. Rising majestically more than 9,200 feet above sea level, its three peaks, with one standing out above the others, were continually covered with snow. Runoff from those snows fed the Jordan River, which ran into the Sea of Galilee more than 20 miles to the south. The mountain was noted for how the sun reflected brilliantly off the glistening snows and how the peaks were often wrapped in clouds that appeared and then dissipated quickly.

Jesus walked with purpose, striding with a strong pace that ate up the 14 miles to the mountain. They walked steadily upward through fragrant fruit orchards and vineyards in the foothills and through heavy woods as they climbed the western slope of the mountain. From time to time they'd stop and look back at the way they had come, admiring a panoramic view that allowed them to see for dozens of miles.

For men who were more accustomed to the rolling instability of a fishing boat, the transition to mountain climber did not come easily. By the time they broke though the tree line toward the top of the mountain, the disciples were wiped out. They stopped to rest, exhausted by the climb yet exhilarated by the view. At times they had shaded their eyes from the brightness of the sun sparkling off the snow and ice above them at the summit, and they enjoyed the increasing coolness as they continued to climb.

Jesus rested with them briefly then ascended a bit higher up the slope. They had seen Him do that before when He went off to pray. Again they had the feeling that He was bearing a heavy weight on His heart, but they still didn't know what to say or do.

For a long time, they watched Jesus at prayer as they had watched Him so many times before. The sun was beginning to cast long shadows down the other side of the peaks, signaling the close of the day. As twilight came, their eyes felt heavy with weariness. The three began to doze as they waited for Jesus to come back to them.

Suddenly they were startled awake by brilliant light above them. What they saw left them in open-mouthed wonder.

Above them was Jesus, different than they'd ever seen Him before. They'd seen Him walk on water and multiply a little boy's lunch into a meal for 5,000 people; but now Jesus was literally glowing with supernatural shining radiance. As they continued to gaze at Him in awe, it occurred to them that the light—so bright that there was no human comparison—was coming from *within* Him, not from an external source. In spite of the dazzling illumination, they did not have to shade their eyes. The light didn't repel their vision; it enhanced it! Years later they could only shake their heads in wonder when they tried to describe the majesty and marvel of that moment.

Then, to only increase their amazement, two men appeared, both reflecting the splendor of Jesus and also glowing with light from within. The two bowed in reverence before Jesus, and Jesus called them each by name—Moses and Elijah! These were two of the greatest leaders in their history! Moses had come down from Mount Sinai to give them the Ten Commandments and lead the children of Israel on their exodus from Egypt. Elijah was regarded as one of the greatest prophets, stopping rain for three years and calling down fire from heaven with his prayers. The conversation that followed suddenly made sense of all the things Jesus had been saying and the weight they could tell He was carrying.

Moses spoke of the Exodus—of how the Lord had supernaturally liberated His people from overwhelming oppression and odds. He spoke of his time on another mountaintop—Mount Sinai—where he had received the Ten Commandments that formed the foundation of the Law. He had been able to give the people God's guidelines for living but had not been able to show them how to have the power to live out those laws. "You," he said to Jesus, with deep respect, "will be the true liberator. With Your exodus from earth, You will make the way possible for all people to find true freedom . . . and You will be able to give them the power to live out God's law from the heart. You are the one I was pointing to all along!"

Then Elijah—the one that many considered the greatest prophet—spoke. "I was able to stand true and speak for God even in the face of the strongest opposition. I could tell people about God, then step back and watch Him work wonders that made people bow low in worship. But worship that depends on wonders doesn't last. I know You will face the ultimate opposition, but You will stay true and take Your stand for God and give Yourself for all people everywhere. When people worship because of what You do for them, it will come because You've worked a wonder in their hearts."

They continued to talk, and it was obvious that the two greatest men in their history were speaking words of encouragement to Jesus about what was awaiting Him; they were sharing with Him the emotional weight of His coming sacrifice on the cross. It was a sacred exchange never to be repeated in human history.

In what seemed to take only a few moments, but later they realized had lasted for hours, the three disciples watched the two visitors from eternity talk with Jesus. For a long time, all they could do was listen in rapt wonder, basking in the majesty of those moments. Finally, Peter found his voice and blurted out Peter-fashion . . .

"T-T-Teacher . . . this is wonderful! I can't believe You'd let us be here with You. I wish this could last forever. Let us make some memorials to this moment—one for You, one for Moses and one for Elijah! We bow before all of you!"

As he spoke, a cloud began to envelop them and the entire mountaintop, and the cloud glowed with light they could not only see but also *feel!* The sense of the awesome Presence intensified. The very air throbbed with supernatural life. John whispered in awe, *"Shekinah..."* They were seeing the actual glory of the Creator and Sustainer of the universe! A voice spoke, regal and deep. *"This is My Son, whom I love. Listen to and obey Him!"* Peter stopped his babbling, and the three disciples fell on their faces, overwhelmed and afraid that they might die in the midst of the majesty.

Then, abruptly, the cloud was gone. The radiant light that had bathed them disappeared, and so did Moses and Elijah. Only Jesus remained, now visible as they had always seen Him, now lit with the growing rays of dawn. They found themselves shaking, and then Jesus was gently helping them up, saying, "It's all right, men, don't be afraid. I told you that you would see the Kingdom in full effect—my glory living through you from the inside out. But don't say anything until I've risen from the dead. Then this will all become clear to you."

They walked down the mountain together . . . Jesus walking with His shoulders squared with renewed determination they hadn't seen the day before, as He began His final, unflinching journey to Jerusalem and a date with destiny on a cross. The disciples whispered among themselves, trying to comprehend their incomprehensible experience.

When they got back Caesarea Philippi, there was a large crowd gathered, milling about in confusion. At the center were the other disciples being harassed by a teacher of the law from the local synagogue and a distraught father pleading for anyone who would listen to help his son.

Jesus smiled and winked at His three companions, then strode into the center of the multitude. Moments later a little boy was free, a father's faith rewarded and masses of people were in awe of Jesus of Nazareth, their lives transformed with new meaning and purpose at seeing the power of God in real life—a day like so many they'd experienced with Jesus before. Standing there, watching Jesus work, the three could only shake their heads again in wonder.

No matter where He might lead, the disciples were determined to follow Jesus. He was the only one who brought purpose and meaning to their lives. He was the only one worth following.

From the majesty of the mountaintop to the lowest valley of human misery, *any* day with Jesus is an adventure, because *anything* is possible with Him!

Anywhere with Jesus can lead to supernatural surprises. It isn't where you're going that matters; it is *Who* you are following. Life is about Jesus being King of the heart and living His life through you from the inside out.

Following Jesus is the only path worth following—the only way life truly has eternal meaning.

I'm following Him wherever He may lead.

How about you?

BEYOND THE STORY
To Help You Think, Pray, Share and Do

1. For a time, Peter was more interested in a spiritual life that brought position and power than suffering and sacrifice. What is most important to you in your spiritual life? Why?

2. Jesus talked about the importance of "living from the inside out." What does living from the inside out mean to you? What difference does it make in the way you live?

3. Peter's misunderstanding of Jesus' mission brought a sharp rebuke from Him. When has the Lord had to correct you in a direct way because you wanted things according to your plan instead of His?

4. Jesus was about to head down the mountain to the lowest possible valley anyone has ever experienced—His sacrificial death on the cross for the sins of the world. At that important moment, God sent two messengers to encourage and strengthen Him. Who has encouraged you in the past at just the right moment? Who have you sought to encourage when they needed support? Look for someone to encourage today.

2

THE JESUS ROAD
(Andrew)

LUKE 9:51-56

The chill of the night air crept in among the group of men, causing them to draw their cloaks more tightly around them. The smell of wood smoke, the crackle of the fire and the cheery light it threw on the circle of faces was reassuring even though they were many miles from home.

Andrew looked across the fire at the face of his Master. Jesus had not joined in the banter they normally shared at the end of each day. He had been unusually quiet and pensive. As the firelight flickered across His features, Andrew smiled at Jesus with a look of love and admiration.

It was more than three years since Andrew first saw the face of the carpenter from Nazareth. Andrew had been following with interest the fiery and unorthodox ministry of a man the people called John the Baptizer. One day, as Andrew was walking with John, the prophet suddenly stopped, staring at an oncoming figure with eyes that burned with passion and awe. Extending an arm bronzed and leathery from extended time in desert sun, he pointed at the man approaching and said, "Behold . . . the Lamb of God who takes away the sins of the world." John spoke with such reverence and awe that Andrew's attention immediately shifted to the one whose face was now clearly visible. What Andrew saw in that face captured his heart from the very beginning.

When Andrew shyly asked where Jesus was staying—a common way of asking to spend time with someone to get to know the person better—Jesus had looked at Andrew with a knowing twinkle in His eyes and a warm smile. His reply was simple: "Come and see." That meeting changed the course of Andrew's life.

Even from their first meeting, there had been something about Jesus that intrigued Andrew. It was an intangible quality that made him want to hear this man's words, made him want to know more about Jesus, made him want to follow Him. The spiritual hunger in Andrew's heart, the questions he had about God . . . As conversations with Jesus turned on the light of revelation for Andrew, it did not take him long to come to the undeniable conclusion that Jesus of Nazareth was more than a carpenter. Indeed, as Andrew heard His words and watched His actions, he knew that Jesus was more than a great teacher, even more than a man among men. Andrew realized that Jesus was the Son of God.

As the conversations continued, Andrew knew that Jesus was doing more than just answering his questions; He was reading Andrew's heart. At a significant pause in the conversation, Jesus leaned forward, looked Andrew in the eyes (it seemed as if He was looking right into Andrew's heart) and simply said, "Follow Me." It was an invitation to a decision. No, it was more than that. Jesus was inviting Andrew to turn his life over to Him and walk His road as His disciple. Outwardly, Andrew nodded as tears filled his eyes. Inwardly, he surrendered his heart. From that moment on, Andrew began to walk the Jesus Road.

The first thing Andrew did after committing himself to Christ was introduce his older brother Peter to Jesus. Peter was the natural leader in the family. He was big, boisterous, impulsive, spontaneous— all the things Andrew was not. Andrew, as the second-born son, had been in the background of Peter's colorful persona since he was born. Compared to Peter, Andrew's personality was about as attractive as the bland sands that made up the Judean wilderness. Yet, in his own quiet way, Andrew began to bring people to meet Jesus.

Like John the Baptizer had said, Andrew wanted Jesus' influence to increase. It didn't matter whether Andrew had any "influence" or not. It was so exciting, so satisfying, so fulfilling to watch other people's lives change after meeting the Master that Andrew started introducing everyone he could to Jesus. It became a way of life for him. In connecting people to Christ, Andrew's heart found its purpose. Andrew decided to spend the rest of his life doing two things: wholeheartedly following Jesus the Christ and helping as many people as he could come to follow Jesus like he did.

The simple fisherman became a fisher of men.

Andrew smiled into the fire. In his mind he walked down a road of memories, reliving the three years he had been a disciple of Jesus. Many times all he could do was marvel at the incredible changes following Jesus had brought to his life. Being on the road with Jesus was an adventure beyond anything a simple man from a small fishing village on the Sea of Galilee could have imagined. Once Andrew said "yes" to Jesus' invitation to follow Him, the entire course of his destiny and eternity turned around. It was a decision he'd never regretted.

Being on the road with Jesus had not always been easy. Jesus had made it clear that being His disciple was not a part-time dalliance; it required full-time devotion. Not everyone in his family or village understood why he gave up the security (and monotony) of the fishing business to follow a teacher with no credentials but Himself. Many nights it would have been far more comfortable to be home and warm in his own bed, in his own house. Yet, the peace resting in Andrew's heart was far better than anywhere he'd ever resided. *Comfort,* Andrew thought to himself wryly, *was not always part of the job description of a disciple of Jesus.* Just being identified as a follower of the Carpenter often brought a range of reactions, from curious skepticism to outright hostility.

People in the mainstream of political power, religious power and social power were initially amused by the Nazarene with His small band of no-name followers; but as word of Jesus' teaching and miracles spread, their reactions became increasingly antagonistic. Jesus was constantly in the intense glare of public media scrutiny. Andrew had never seen anyone more misrepresented and falsely accused. Yet, Andrew never saw his Master respond in an ungracious or improper way. Many times, Jesus actually reached out redemptively to those who criticized Him most vocally. Jesus' ability to deal with the worst side of humanity was beyond what any human could do. *It was,* Andrew thought, *nothing short of supernatural.*

Supernatural. That was the other side of being on the road with Jesus. Whenever Jesus taught God's Word, truth came alive, stimulating Andrew's mind and stirring his emotions. Even more, when Jesus taught, His words were like fresh water on the parched ground of Andrew's spirit. Jesus spoke the Word of God as if He had written it

Himself. No one can communicate the content of written material better than the author. The way Jesus handled the eternal truths of Scripture made Andrew sure that somehow those words were birthed from Jesus' own heart.

Beyond His teaching, Andrew had been awed time and time again by the power Jesus had to completely transform human lives. People warped by sin were renewed to spiritual health by a word of forgiveness. People wracked by physical illness were restored to physical wholeness by a word of healing. People wrapped in the bondage of demonic oppression were released by a word of authority. Faces and places of people forever changed by meeting Jesus flashed across Andrew's mind. Yet, in spite of all the miracles and messages Jesus had brought to the people of Palestine, it always seemed He was living for a bigger, more far-reaching purpose. Andrew was not sure where on their journey they would find that ultimate purpose of Jesus, but he knew he'd walk with Jesus no matter where the road might take them.

It had only been three years . . . Andrew was looking forward to many more years of being on the road with Jesus. The best, he was sure, was yet to come.

The snap of a log on the fire and its upward spray of sparks brought Andrew out of his reminiscing. There was something in Jesus' face that made Andrew lean forward and look more closely at Him. The Master's eyes had a faraway look. For a moment, He seemed to be listening . . . communing with His Father in silent conversation. Andrew always marveled at how Jesus lived in constant communion with His heavenly Father, no matter what the circumstances around Him. The Son and the Father were in unbroken communication and complete agreement at all times.

Then, appearing to reach a conclusion, the muscles in Christ's face tightened. His strong features took on a hardness—a kind of determination—that made Andrew wonder what enemy the Master was preparing to confront and conquer. Andrew had seen that resolute, almost fierce look on Christ's face when the Master dealt with hardened hearts, hypocritical men, disease and demonic powers. What was the Lord looking ahead to now?

The look in Christ's eyes softened. It seemed to Andrew that Jesus was now looking past the unseen enemy ahead to something that made Him eager with anticipation. If Andrew hadn't known better, he'd have thought Christ was happy with the prospect of going home.

Jesus looked up from the fire and gazed around at the group of disciples with tenderness. "Men," He said, "tomorrow, I am going to Jerusalem."

There was such a sense of finality in His voice that it brought them all to captivated attention. For a moment no one spoke as each man struggled to decipher the meaning behind the tone of Jesus' voice. Finally Peter ventured, "What do you mean, Lord? We know it is time for the Feast of Passover in Jerusalem. Is that why we're going?"

Jesus smiled a sad smile at them. "No, men, it's time for me to go there to accomplish that for which I was born. The Son of Man must suffer many things and be rejected by the elders, chief priests and teachers of the law, and He must be killed and on the third day be raised to life. If any of you want to follow me, you must deny yourself and take up your cross and follow me. Whoever wants to save his life will lose it, but whoever loses his life for me will save it. You'll never regret following me. But tomorrow I head for Jerusalem."

Then it hit the men. What Jesus was really saying was that He was walking His final road. A cross awaited Him in Jerusalem. He was going to Jerusalem to die.

There was little conversation the rest of the night.

The next day, Jesus set out on a course in a straight line for Jerusalem. There was just one problem in His plan—it would take them right through Samaria.

There was little courtesy and less love between the Samaritans— a mixed race ethnically and religiously—and the Jewish people. Going through Samaria on the way to a Jewish religious feast not only could be uncomfortable, but it could also be dangerous. Threats, beatings and worse were not uncommon to those unfortunate Jews who ventured through Samaritan land. When the disciples politely suggested they would be better off taking a detour around Samaria, Jesus merely shook His head and continued walking toward Jerusalem.

Andrew tried to make sense of the events around the campfire from the previous night. What did Christ mean? As he walked under the warmth of the Samaritan sun, the words of Isaiah the prophet came back to him—words that had been recorded 700 years before suddenly came to life and made sense to him.

The Sovereign Lord has opened my ears, and I have not been rebellious; I have not drawn back. I offered my back to those who beat me, my cheeks to those who pulled out my beard; I did not hide my face from mocking and spitting. Because the Sovereign Lord helps me, I will not be disgraced. Therefore have I set my face like flint, and I know I will not be put to shame.

Startled, Andrew turned to look at Jesus. The set of Christ's jaw, the determination in His eyes, the rock-hard resolve in His face all became superimposed over Isaiah's words. What Andrew heard in Isaiah's words and saw in Jesus' face made him instinctively sense they were headed for the pivotal point in human history. He tried to say something to Jesus to let Him know that he understood, but the lump in his throat choked off anything he attempted to say. Andrew was beginning to understand the bigger purpose Jesus was living for. As his understanding grew, a tear left a lonely streak in the dust on his cheek at the thought of what might be in store for his Master.

As the sun descended toward the horizon, they came to the outskirts of a Samaritan village. Turning to James and John, Jesus instructed them to see if there was lodging and food available for their group for the night. They would wait and rest while the two brothers went on ahead.

It wasn't but a short time later that James and John came rapidly up the trail to them. Their steps were stiff and short, their faces flushed and red.

"Do you know what those miserable Samaritans said to us?" John exploded. His eyes blazed with anger. "The minute they found out who we were and that we were headed for Jerusalem, they told us to get out of town or they would beat us."

"Not only that," James added, his voice trembling with rage, "even when we told them we were with Jesus of Nazareth, they refused us. They said they had heard of His teaching and miracles but would have nothing to do with Him if He was going to go to Jerusalem. Master, they said they would accept you if you would accept their ways. They would not accept yours."

"How could they treat us this way?" John railed. "How could they treat *you* this way, Lord?" John thrust an accusing finger back toward the village. "They have rejected God. They deserve God's judgment. Shall we call down fire on them? Let's give them what they deserve."

Jesus looked steadily at the two brothers, who at that moment certainly reflected the nickname He had given them. The "Sons of Thunder" were ready to call down some lightning and scorch the Samaritans into oblivion. Jesus' tone was one of rebuke mixed with disappointment. *"You do not know what kind of spirit you are of, for the Son of Man did not come to destroy men's lives, but to save them."*

The two brothers, so flushed with hurt pride thinly disguised as righteous indignation a moment ago, were suddenly deflated. They stood silently, looking at the ground in chagrin and embarrassment.

Watching that exchange between the Master and James and John, understanding came to Andrew as to why they had gone through Samaria. Other than the fact that Jesus would accept no detours on the road to the cross, Andrew saw Jesus reach out a hand of redemptive friendship to even those who were considered His enemies. The sacrifice He was going to make would be for *all* people, even for those who would choose to reject Him. The road of redemption Jesus was preparing was for an entire world, not just one small group among all the nations of earth.

Andrew's vision had been so limited. The purpose of Jesus was far bigger than he could have imagined. No matter what tribe, color, language, Christ was making the road for every person to come home to God the Father. It began to make sense now. Beyond the agony of the cross was a redemptive invitation to join Him in heaven. Andrew's eyes shone with admiration as he looked at Jesus. What a man! What a Savior!

Without another word, Jesus turned and strode purposefully down the road toward His date with destiny in Jerusalem.

For a moment Andrew watched and then he turned and followed in the footsteps of Jesus. Wherever those footsteps might lead, Andrew was going too. He'd made his choice of what road he would walk no matter what.

The Jesus Road was his road.

Is it yours?

BEYOND THE STORY
To Help You Think, Pray, Share and Do

1. When you think of Jesus, what words come to mind? Why? Why do you think most people form the opinions of Christ that they do?

2. An old saying reminds us, *"Choose your path wisely . . . you'll wake up in it in 20 years."* How would you describe the path you've been walking? How much of it has become a rut? What might Jesus be saying to you about getting out of your current path to walk in His?

3. What does walking the "Jesus Road" mean to you? As you read about the strength and determination of Christ headed toward His date with destiny on the cross, how did it bolster your resolve to walk with Him no matter where the Road may lead?

4. How are you seeking to help others walk the Jesus Road with you?

3

ARRIVAL OF THE KING

(Palm Sunday)

MATTHEW 21:1-10

It had been building for weeks.

He heard it every time news from Jerusalem reached their group as they continued on the road to the City of David. The word was that the Pharisees had decided the Carpenter from Nazareth was a danger to the nation, and plans to entrap and condemn Him were being formulated. For nearly three years now the religious leaders had been criticizing, questioning and dogging Jesus' steps as He walked, taught and transformed lives throughout Israel. They were infuriated by His words, bewildered by His power and threatened by His increasing popularity among the people. Pressure from that quarter had become so strong that it was nearly tangible.

For His part, Jesus felt an increasing sense of resolution. At night He had begun to tell His followers that He was going to Jerusalem to be betrayed, condemned and crucified by the religious leaders there. As the firelight flickered on His face, He would sometimes get a faraway look in His eyes, as if He were homesick. Sometimes the muscles in His jaw tightened and His eyes sparked with a determination His disciples had seen before when He confronted dark forces. It seemed, indeed, that things were building to a climax. Passover was one of the most important religious times of the year in Jerusalem—a festival that brought more than two million people to its gates.

The disciples had tried to discourage Jesus from putting Himself in needless danger. When He had described His impending death, Peter had even tried to talk Him out of such a possibility. Jesus' response had surprised and shocked them all when He sharply rebuked Peter with the words, "Get behind me, Satan." It was clear that for

Jesus there was no turning back. He was a man on a mission, and His mission was almost over.

Sunday had dawned clear and bright in the village of Bethany, just two miles from Jerusalem. Jesus and His disciples had spent the night there, visiting their old friends Mary, Martha and their brother, Lazarus, who had become a focal point in the controversy. When you get raised from the dead, you tend to draw attention.

They spent the first part of the day enjoying the company of their friends. Jesus laughed and talked with them, but there was an undeniable sense that He knew He would not be back to visit again. Late in the morning, He turned to two of His disciples and asked them to go on an errand for Him. Not far away, He said, they would find a donkey colt tied up next to its mother. They were to untie the colt and bring it with its mother. If anyone asked them what they were doing, they were to say, "The Lord has need of it."

They found the colt and its mother tied up just as He had said. As they began to untie the animals, a man came out of his house and said, "What are you doing? Those are my donkeys." They replied, "The Lord has need of them." For a brief moment the man weighed their words. Then he smiled and said, "If the Lord needs them, they're yours. Take them. God bless you."

When they returned to Jesus, He gathered everyone together and looked at them for a long moment, then said, "It's time to go to Jerusalem."

As they approached the city, one of His followers suggested they come in by a back route to avoid attention. Instead, Jesus chose the road that led around the south side of the Mount of Olives, a popular area for people to gather for picnics and outings. Given that Passover was beginning, it would be one of the most crowded areas in the whole countryside.

The afternoon sun was shining brightly as they finally saw the outline of the capital city of their nation. The road wound down the mount and through the beautiful park-like area dotted with palm trees and other greenery and then across an open plain before entering the city through the eastern gate.

Just as they got to the crest of the hill, and before starting their descent, Jesus stopped and looked across the Kidron Valley at Jerusalem.

The Temple shone in the bright sunlight, plainly visible against the backdrop of other buildings, homes, shops and winding streets. The Master sighed heavily and then suddenly began to weep. Deep sobs shook His shoulders. For a moment, all that His disciples could do was stare as they watched tears run down His cheeks and onto His beard.

Speaking hoarsely through His tears, Jesus said, "Oh, Jerusalem, Jerusalem . . . how often I wanted to gather you under my care like a mother hen gathers her chicks, but you wouldn't let me! Now, because you chose to go it on your own, everything will be destroyed . . . and it didn't need to happen . . ." For a few more moments, Jesus wept; and then, drying the tears from His sun-bronzed face, He said, "Bring the colt here to me, please."

The colt had never been ridden. Jesus gently took its furry nose in His hands and patted it as if to reassure it. Then, taking His cloak and putting it over the back of the colt, He got on its back. The colt turned its head to look at who had mounted it, and seeing Jesus, stood quietly as if waiting for a signal from its Master.

Suddenly words from Scripture dawned on the small group surrounding Jesus, and the impact was electrifying. The words of the ancient prophet came to them as if prompted by the Spirit of God: "Tell the daughter of Zion [the name for Jerusalem], 'Behold, your King is coming to you, Humble, and sitting on a donkey, and a colt, the foal of a donkey.' "

When a king entered a city, he could do it in one of two ways—he could ride a white horse to let the people know he was prepared for battle and ready to go to war, or he could ride a donkey as a sign that he was returning victorious from the battle and had secured the peace. In this simple act of riding the colt, Jesus was making an undeniable statement that He was entering Jerusalem as a king of peace.

Word that Jesus was entering Jerusalem as a king began to spread through the crowds of people around the Mount of Olives, rippling out to the city's narrow streets, shops and homes and generated increasing excitement. Women who stood in the doorways of their homes and then gathered their children around them began to head toward the place where history was being made. Men stopped working, leaving projects unfinished, as a higher priority took precedence. Storekeepers listened to the news and then shut down their businesses. No one was there to buy from them anyway. It seemed that the whole city, already overfilled with holiday pilgrims, was streaming out of the eastern gate to see what was going on.

As they reached the procession, all attention focused on Jesus atop the colt. He acknowledged the people not as a politician glad-handing all He met but as a king acknowledging the people He rightfully ruled and loved.

The scene was a kaleidoscope of color, sound and energy generated by a crowd caught up in the power of a strategic moment. Thousands, then tens of thousands strained to see the Man from Galilee as He arrived in the city. As if by an unspoken signal, people began to lay their coats on the road in front of the colt, forming a new road paved with acts of adoration and submission to a king. Young men shinnied up palm trees and cut off palm branches, throwing them to the crowd below. Now palm fronds and coats formed a regal highway for Jesus as the colt slowly parted the teeming mass of people.

Faces glowed with excitement and conversations buzzed as people inquired and were told what was happening. Small children clung to their parents' garments, not completely understanding what was going on, but trying to see through the forest of adults to catch a glimpse of the man on the colt. Dogs ran back and forth around the outside of the crowd, barking noisily, stirred by the emotions they sensed from the huge crowd.

Then a voice off to the left shouted, "Hosanna! Save us!" Suddenly the words spread through the crowd until it seemed the unspoken yearning of a nation that had been under the bondage of Roman domination—all their frustration and pent-up longing to be free— came bursting out as cries of adoration and supplication: "Hosanna to the Son of David! Blessed is He who comes in the name of the Lord! Hosanna in the highest!"

Their words recognized Jesus as the one who could set them free, as the rightful king of their nation, as their deliverer; and in their worship there was also the pleading for Him to step forward and drive their enemies out of the land.

In the midst of this thrilling symphony of human enthusiasm, a small group of dark-robed men elbowed their way through the crowd, anger flashing from their eyes. The religious leaders had also heard what was going on, and they could not tolerate a simple carpenter from a backwoods town recognized as the Son of David, a king! *Their* king.

Shaking their fists at Jesus, one of them angrily demanded, "Stop this! Tell these people to stop this! This is not right! We have not sanctioned this!"

Jesus gazed steadily at them and then suddenly smiled. Raising His voice so that it could be heard above the crowd, He shouted back, "If I told these people to be quiet, the stones would begin to take their place in shouting their praises! You can't stop what God has begun."

With those words the men, eyes burning with hatred and backs stiff with indignation, pulled their robes tightly around themselves and walked away, trying to ignore the exuberant crowd. Meanwhile, the celebration continued until Jesus entered the eastern gate of the city and continued on to the Temple.

It is a day forever etched in history. We now know it as Palm Sunday and talk about it as the Triumphal Entry. Once you know the full impact of all that was going on as Jesus made His entrance into the city of Jerusalem that first Palm Sunday, your understanding of who Jesus is and what His claims are for our lives becomes undeniable.

What is even more powerful than the reception Jesus received as He began the countdown of the most important week in human history is that when He left the city out of the western gate the following Friday, carrying a cross, and now mocked by that same crowd, He was doing what only a king can do for His people. He was laying down His life so that when we receive Him as King of our hearts, we someday can have a triumphal entry into another city—the city of heaven.

BEYOND THE STORY
To Help You Think, Pray, Share and Do

1. Being a follower of Jesus has always been controversial. Why do you think He generates such controversy?

2. Jesus' entrance into Jerusalem started with tears as He wept over the city, and then brought great cheers as a huge crowd gathered to welcome Him. Often there's a big difference between people who are caught up in the excitement of a crowd praising Jesus and being a truly committed disciple of Jesus. What are some of the ways you can tell the difference?

3. On Sunday, the crowd wanted to crown Jesus as their king. On Friday, they wanted to see Him crucified. How could things change so dramatically in such a short time? Why do you think people still behave like that today?

4. For every one verse about the first coming of Jesus, there are eight verses about His second coming. What are you doing to prepare for His second coming . . . when He arrives as the conquering King of all?

4

LIFE LESSONS FROM AN UPPER ROOM

(The Last Supper)

JOHN 13:1-30

Night was coming.

Jerusalem was swollen with tens of thousands of pilgrims assembled to celebrate the Passover feast. Most had settled in for the night, but there were those who rested uneasy, sensing a gathering storm, unseen but nonetheless real. The night sky was clear, but the darkness was heavy and close. Dogs looked upward, then cowered, whining softly as they sensed things unable to be heard by human ears. Those with hearts tuned to the Spirit of God listened intently and began to pray, heeding a call to intercede intensely.

Time was moving toward its close . . . and its beginning . . . arriving at a date with destiny that would forever mark recorded history.

In an upper room in one of the many stone houses in the city, a group of men were gathered in heavy-hearted silence. They had been that way all day—moody, grouchy, overly sensitive. An argument had broken out among them when the mother of James and John had the audacity to ask Jesus if her two sons could have the seats of authority on His right and left hand when He took His kingdom throne. Jesus' response was grim. He told her that she had no idea what she was asking . . . no idea what the price would be for Him to return to His throne and His home in heaven.

The incident had set them off. Unspoken agendas and unholy attitudes came to the surface as unseemly behavior—scowling and sniping at each other as outward evidences of anger boiling just under the surface.

Jesus had surprised them by saying He had arranged for the Passover meal. They were to look for a man carrying a water pot—odd, because that was a woman's job—and follow the man to the appointed place. They were so wrapped up in their own feelings that they were oblivious to the heart of their Teacher and His own needs.

This was Jesus' last night on earth. He had looked forward to this night with the twelve men He had chosen three years ago—to be with Him, to learn from Him, to minister with Him, to carry on His work when His mission was done. These were His disciples, His chosen friends, His intimate companions. This meal was to become far more than a normal Passover feast . . . it was His last supper with them and the beginning of a new way to remember His sacrifice for all time to come.

If ever Jesus needed His men to support Him, it was now.

Unfortunately, the disciples were preoccupied with their squabbling. As they entered the room, each man looked away from a clay pot of water standing near the door. They all knew it was there; similar jars stood by nearly every door in every home in Israel. What they didn't want to acknowledge was what the jar of water stood for, because it beckoned them to humility and servanthood.

Almost all travel was by foot over dusty roads, and the footwear of the day was open sandals; so walking was a dirty, dusty endeavor. As guests entered a home, it was the job of a servant to wash the travel grit off of the feet of all who entered the home. It was a menial, dirty job that only a lowly servant would do. To enter a home with unwashed feet was beyond impolite; it was downright rude.

However, at this Passover supper there was no servant to wash their feet, and no one wanted to take on such a role, especially when they had all been arguing and jockeying for positions of power. As they gathered around the low table, reclining on their left sides so they could eat with their right hands, they stretched out their robes to cover their feet—trying to pretend nothing was wrong when, in fact, everything was.

They looked toward the table, low to the ground and U-shaped so that three could recline at the bottom of the U and up to five could recline on either spur. Even now they were edgy about who got to sit where, since *where* you sat in social settings said a lot about *who* you were in terms of status and significance. Still scowling at each other, they silently jockeyed for the best positions around the table.

Jesus shook His head as He watched them. He let them finally find their places at the table and whispered to Judas to take the place to His left, a place reserved for someone special. If the disciples had looked closely, they would have seen the strain of His impending trial and death weighing on Him; they would have seen His knowing look of disappointment over their immature squabbling; they would have seen His love for them overcoming all else.

But they were unwilling to look at each other or look up at Jesus . . . or at the water pot by the door, which seemed to grow larger and more imposing by the minute.

For a long moment no one said anything in the heavy silence. They hoped no one would notice, and the Passover meal could begin, dirty feet and all.

The Passover meal was a central tradition in their spiritual life as a nation. It was a yearly event so important that children began memorizing each part of the ceremony, every passage of Scripture, emphasizing the historical and spiritual essentials for them to remember. The Passover meal was called the *Seder*, meaning to "set order," because there was a distinct order to everything they did—15 consecutive steps constituted a full Seder. They knew the steps by heart, even if at this moment their hearts were not in it.

There were several vital elements to the meal, including the Feast of Unleavened Bread, which had started days before. The Feast of Unleavened Bread brought them back to some powerful historical lessons from God's deliverance of their nation from slavery in Egypt, and some important spiritual directives to help them be free from sin now.

Yeast was a sign of the contamination that sin brought to a person's life. Even a little leavening (a little yeast) would soon work its influence in the rest of the bread, just as a little sin would soon infect the whole of a person's life. When they'd left Egypt, the Lord had commanded them to eat and bring only unleavened bread with them. Any connection to the corrupting influence of the bondage of sin in Egypt was to be left behind. The present-day equivalent was to cleanse their homes from every vestige of leaven to signify a clean break from the past and a fresh start free from contamination. The obvious inference

was that people would ask the Lord to cleanse their hearts from the
selfishness of sin in the same way.

With that cleansing of house and heart in mind, the other components of the Seder were to both remind and release other spiritual lessons.

The lamb was to remind them of how the blood of spotless lambs
smeared over the Israelites' doorposts had protected them from the
Angel of Death; that blood was their salvation as judgment passed
over them.

Every person had to sacrifice his own lamb at the Temple as a reminder of the intensely personal nature of sin and its consequences.
After the blood was captured by the priest, the lamb was prepared for
roasting over a fire at home. The lamb had a wooden spit running
through its mouth on one end and the tail at the other, with another
stick against the ribs to prop it open. The two wooden pieces formed
a cross.

The unleavened bread was to remind them of the haste in which
they left slavery behind on that first exodus from Egypt.

The bowl of salt water was to remind them of the tears shed as
slaves in Egypt and the waters of the Red Sea, which God had parted
for them so they could cross safely on dry ground and walk toward
the Promised Land.

The bitter herbs of horseradish and lettuce were to be eaten with
the unleavened bread to remind them of the bitter taste that slavery
left in their mouths.

The Charoset paste—a brown mush made of apples, dates, pome-
granates and cinnamon—was to remind them of the clay from which
they made bricks in Egypt.

Four cups of wine, drunk at different parts of the Feast, each represented the redemption promise of Yahweh their Deliverer, recorded in
Exodus 6:6-7. Together the four cups were called the Cup of Salvation.

"*I will bring you out* from under the burdens of the Egyptians." The
First Cup of Holiness represented separation from sin, and sanctifica-
tion or purification of heart.

"*I will rescue you* from their bondage." The Second Cup of Explain-
ing or Proclaiming told the great story of God's deliverance and was
rehearsed for young and old alike.

"I will redeem you . . ." This was the Third Cup of Redemption and Thanksgiving.

"I will take you as my people and I will be your God." This was the Fourth Cup of Completion and Commitment.

The Master of the Meal would begin by lifting the First Cup and proclaiming a blessing. Jesus took the first cup and tenderly looked around the table at His men. They'd been with Him for three years. He'd poured Himself into them, showing them by His own life what life was supposed to be like for them.

He said, "I have deeply desired to eat this Passover with you before I suffer. I tell you . . . I won't eat it again until what this means is fulfilled in the Kingdom of God." He lifted it up with both hands and began the familiar words . . .

"Blessed are You, Lord our God, King of the Universe, who creates the fruit of the vine . . .

Blessed are You, Lord our God, King of the Universe, who has chosen us from among all nations, exalted us above all tongues, and sanctified us with His commandments. With love You have given us, O Lord our God, appointed times for gladness, festivals and seasons for rejoicing, this Feast of Unleavened Bread, the season of our deliverance, with love, a sacred rehearsal in remembrance of the departure from Egypt. For You have chosen us, and You have sanctified us from all the nations, and You have given us festivals with gladness as our heritage. Blessed are You, Lord our God, who sanctifies Israel and the seasons . . ."

These were the familiar, sacred words spoken just as they were supposed to be, and the disciples responded as they had been taught: "Blessed are You, Lord our God, King of the Universe, who has kept us alive, sustained us and brought us to this season."

With those familiar words, the tension eased a bit. Perhaps the debacle of the dirty feet had been forgotten.

The next Seder step was the washing of the hands by the host. Three times, in a prescribed way, the water was used to cleanse the host's hands as he prepared to have the rest of the meal served.

It was at that point that Jesus went completely off script and taught them one of the life lessons of the Upper Room they would never forget.

Jesus walked over to the doorway, took off His outer garment and wrapped a towel around His waist, then poured water into a basin. Carrying the basin over to the table, Jesus knelt before His men and began to do the thing no one else wanted to do.

He began to wash the disciples' feet, and He did it because He was the Son of God.

He started with Peter, who was at one end of the U. When Peter saw Jesus kneel in front of him, he drew his feet even further under his robe, his eyes flashing protest and embarrassment. "Lord, You're not going to wash my feet, are You?" They all knew it was forbidden to force a servant to do the lowly job of washing his master's feet . . . and here the master wanted to wash his feet!

Jesus looked up and smiled as He continued to pour water into the basin. "Peter, you don't understand what I'm doing right now, but someday you will."

Peter shook his head emphatically and said, "No! You'll never wash my feet! You're the Master . . . the host . . . this just isn't done! Someone of Your stature should never stoop to such a thing! I'll never let You do it!"

This time Jesus met Peter's eyes and held them, his expression sad but steady.

"Peter, if you don't let me wash you, you have no part with me—you'll not belong to me."

Suddenly Peter realized that Jesus was talking about more than dusty feet. He'd exposed Peter's dirty motives. Beneath that feigned humility was a desire to be first, to stand out. If following the way of Jesus meant relinquishing that drive to stand above the rest, then his dedication to a self-first desire had just led to a parting of the ways. Dirty feet weren't the point; a divided heart was the issue. It was a matter of inner holiness, not outer hygiene, and that issue made all the difference between belonging to Jesus or not.

When Peter realized what was really going on, his eyes welled up with tears at the thought of what he'd almost done. He threw back his robe and thrust his feet forward, leaning forward to show the top of his balding head at the same time.

"Then, please," he said meekly, fervently, "don't wash only my feet, Lord. Wash my hands and head too." The invitation flowed from his desperation for total interior cleansing, not just a partial, outward ritual.

Jesus took the towel, soaked it with water and playfully rubbed the top of Peter's head. Smiles around the room acknowledged their understanding and assent. They, too, wanted what Peter had asked for.

Jesus said, "A person who has been fully cleansed doesn't need to take a complete bath again. He just needs to make sure he frequently washes off the dirt of the outside world. And you are clean . . ."

Jesus paused, glancing toward the head of the table where Judas reclined. "But that isn't true of everyone here." With that, He finished washing the now humble Peter's feet.

Jesus knelt before each beloved disciple, one by one, and washed each man's feet. The room was silent except for the splashing and sloshing of water as a towel was squeezed, scrubbed and soaked . . . squeezed, scrubbed and soaked.

These were sacred moments. Once again Jesus had turned conventional wisdom and tradition on its head and made everyone focus on the central issue of the condition of the heart. They'd seen Him do it so many times over the three years they had been with Him. He never violated any of God's laws, but always reminded them of what the spirit of those laws was really all about: mercy over rigidity; forgiveness over form; relationship over ritual; the internal over the external; holy love over hard-line law.

He washed every foot, seeming to take extra care with Judas's. Then He threw out the dirty water, hung the towel back on its peg and replaced the basin. He put on His robe and returned to the table to recline again.

He looked around the room, each disciple leaning forward in anticipation. The unbroken tradition of the Seder had been changed; a new way had begun.

There was a hint of urgency in Jesus' voice as He said, "Do you understand what I've done for you? You call me 'Teacher' and 'Lord,' and you are right . . . that's who I am. And since I am your teacher and Lord, and I have washed your feet, you ought to wash each other's feet. I have given you an example to follow. Do for others what I've done for you. It is true that a servant is not greater than the master. Nor are messengers more important than the one who sends the message. You know these things—now do them! That is the path of blessing."

A look of sadness came to His face, and for a moment the Lord appeared to weigh His words carefully. "I am not saying these things to all of you; I know each of you that I've chosen so well. The Scriptures say, 'The one who shares my food has raised his heel against me . . . he's turned against me.' This will come true tonight. But I'm telling you all this now so that when it happens you'll remember and believe that I really am the Messiah. The truth is that anyone who welcomes my messenger is welcoming me; and anyone who welcomes me is welcoming the Father who sent me."

It looked like His great heart was about to break with anguish and sorrow when He said . . .

"One of you is going to betray me."

For an instant, they were stunned; things had turned from sacred to shocking in a sentence.

Their response was instinctive and explosive. Angry, surprised, bewildered, protective . . . they didn't know what to feel or quite what to say. They all talked over the top of each other, asking the same question out loud and the same question in their minds.

"Lord, it's not me, is it?"

"Who is it? We're going to kill him!"

Around and across the table they continued to question Him vehemently, but Jesus was silent. It was obvious that He knew who the traitor was, and He wasn't telling. Why wouldn't He let them do something? All it took was one word, but Jesus seemed to know that bigger things were going on. He always did.

John leaned back and asked Jesus something, and the Lord whispered something back. Then Jesus took a piece of bread, dipped it in the bitter herbs and fed it to Judas, saying something to him that the rest couldn't hear. But the look that passed between them was tender and terrible at the same time. Judas stood suddenly, wrapped his robe tightly around himself and hurried from the room.

Still the disciples continued to ask Jesus what He meant . . . and then to argue. *Who would do such a thing?! I wouldn't . . . but you might. I've been with Jesus longer . . . I know Him better than you . . . I'm closer to Him than you . . . I've done more for Him that you . . .*

I'm greater than you!

What had started as righteous indignation focused on protecting Jesus devolved into a debate over who had the greatest reputation. Voices grew louder, hands flailed wildly, fingers pointed accusingly . . .

Jesus let them rant. Finally, He held up His hands to stop them and they leaned back, huffing, each trying to get the last word in like little boys in a family spat.

It occurred to them then what fools they were making of themselves. If anyone ever wrote about their behavior this night, they were going to look shallow and self-absorbed when their Savior needed them most.

Jesus leaned in again, as if trying to emphasize a point. "In this world the kings and great men order their people around and yet they want to have the title of 'friends of the people.' But it can't be like that among you. With you it's got to be different. The highest needs to become the lowest . . . the master choosing to become a servant. Who would you rather be, the important person sitting at the head of the table being served by others, or the servant doing all the work? The obvious answer is to be the important person, but I have chosen to be your servant. That's the leadership I want you to have." His eyes were intent, His voice low but insistent. They had to get this . . . they had to!

He looked at them as one appreciates the loving investment of long-time friends.

"You are the ones who stood by me through everything, through my trials . . . and just as my Father has granted me a Kingdom, I now grant you the right to eat and drink at my table in the Kingdom. And one day you will sit on thrones judging the twelve tribes of Israel." He smiled, looking ahead at things to come.

The Seder continued, falling back into its familiar rhythm.

Jesus took a piece of the flat, crisp unleavened bread, retrieving it from the folds of a linen napkin where it had been wrapped. He broke it in two, the snapping sound sharp in the room. One piece was put back in the napkin, the other shrouded in another linen napkin and given to one of the participants to hide somewhere in the room. (When children were present, they would make a game of finding the hidden bread, retrieving it and resurrecting it for all to see. Before the meal could continue, they would have to find the buried bread that symbolically represented the Passover Lamb.)

Jesus and the disciples continued their Seder, the symbols and story interwoven so that with all five senses they could experience again the remarkable, supernatural history of their national redemption.

When they came to the meal portion of the Seder, Jesus again took them away from their familiar history to help them more fully understand their future destiny as disciples. He was going home; but He was also the way for all to get to His Father's house. He'd not leave them as orphans when He left, but He'd send another Comforter just like Him to teach, remind, protect, purify and empower them for the big task ahead of them. They listened as they chewed, trying to savor every bite in their mouths and every word in their minds. They'd be digesting the spiritual food He was feeding them for a long time.

Finally the meal was over, and they gave the task of finding the buried bread to the youngest disciple, who sheepishly obliged, handing it to Jesus.

When Jesus took the bread from its linen shroud, He held it up and gave thanks. It looked like ordinary matzo bread with its many pierced holes and multiple stripes; but as Jesus broke it again and began to pass it around to them, what He said next forever changed the meaning of that bread.

"This is my body, given for you. Do this in remembrance of me."

The bread . . . His body? Remember Him? He'd talked openly and often in recent days about what was going to happen, and they still didn't understand. Later, the bread with holes imprinted with stripes would connect to their comprehension when they compared His pierced holy body striped with blood from scourging, and the words that Isaiah wrote centuries before came into focus as images of Calvary were laid on top of the echoes of Passover.

But He was pierced for our transgressions, He was crushed for our iniquities; the punishment that bought us peace was upon Him . . . and by His wounds we are healed.

A series of blessings followed, again in familiar fashion. Blessings from the Psalms for their deliverance; for the food; for living in the land God had promised them so long ago; for Jerusalem; for the meaning of this feast.

They received the blessings, repeated them, relished again the reminders of revelation and redemption.

It was time for the third cup now, the Cup of Redemption and Thanksgiving. Jesus again turned history into destiny. He blessed it and said, "Drink from it, all of you. This is my blood, which seals the covenant. It is poured out for many for the forgiveness of sins. Mark my words, from this moment on I won't drink of this fruit of the vine until that day when I drink it in a new way in my Father's kingdom with you."

He'd taken national history and used it to point to His true identity. Those memories made from a meal were the markers of His mission. The Seder had taught them to look back in gratitude for God's saving power in the past. Jesus had turned the familiar Seder that beckoned them to look back at Passover lambs and what they had done for their nation one fateful night . . . but from now on they would never celebrate the occasion without focusing on what the Lamb of God did to bring salvation to the entire world.

Passover lamb . . . Lamb of God.

Broken unleavened bread . . . Jesus' broken, sinless body.

Blood red wine symbolic of repeated animal sacrifices . . . rich, real blood sacrificed once for all by the Son of God.

National exodus from slavery . . . personal emancipation from sin.

Victory over Pharaoh . . . supremacy over sin, death, Satan and hell.

Promised land . . . the Father's house.

History . . . destiny.

It would all make sense later, as so much of this memorable night in the Upper Room would. But it would take the cleansing and filling of the Holy Spirit for it to become clear to them, and He'd empower them to help others understand too. The life lessons of that Upper Room still teach and transform us today.

John says that Jesus loved His disciples to the end, showing them the full extent of His love.

That lowly, loving deed expressed in all its loneliness the glory and humility of the King who led by making Himself a Servant; the Teacher who taught by living out His own lessons; the Savior who saved by making Himself the sacrifice.

It is a love that keeps on loving, no matter how it is treated . . . a love that can't be broken or defeated.

Those lessons still set the standard for every disciple of Jesus who is called to spiritual leadership. The life lessons of the basin and the towel, the bread and the blood, humility and servanthood, forgiveness in the face of betrayal, unselfish love, sacrifice and salvation.

If we do not learn those lessons, we cannot have His ministry.

When we learn them and live like our Master, our message makes sense to everyone we influence so that Jesus can turn their history into His destiny.

BEYOND THE STORY
To Help You Think, Pray, Share and Do

1. Jesus modeled that great leadership starts with willing servant-hood—just the opposite of the way leadership was viewed then and now. What does the lesson of the basin and towel teach you about true leadership?

2. Jesus took a familiar tradition and turned it into a powerful new revelation about who He is and what He came to earth to do. When has He taken something familiar to you and met you in a fresh way that changed the way you see Him and His mission?

3. What new insights did you learn in this retelling of the first "Last Supper"?

4. The next time you take communion, take an extra moment to remember how the Jewish Passover Seder foretold Christ's death and resurrection. Pray for the Lord to help Jewish people recognize their true Messiah through the Scriptures and traditions.

5

NIGHT OF BETRAYAL
(Judas)

MATTHEW 26:47-56; 27:3-10; LUKE 22:1-6; JOHN 13:21-30

It wasn't supposed to end like this.

He stood alone at the edge of the precipice, his eyes wild and un-worldly, his body trembling, his breath coming in ragged, wheezing, whimpering gasps. His hands tightly clutched one end of his money belt, the other end of the belt was tied to the limb of the tree that stretched out over the Valley of Hinnom below. Voices shouted at him from all directions—taunting, accusing, leering, laughing, pushing. Just one step into oblivion and it would all be over. The voices urged him on with fiendish delight, reveling in the sacrifice he was about to make . . . to them.

It wasn't supposed to end like this.

This was supposed to be the day his greatest dreams came true—his secret longings for himself and his nation gloriously coming to triumphant fruition. But everything was imploding—his expectations, his motivation and the manipulations he'd thought so securely under his direction had spun uncontrollably out of reach. His scheming, se-cret strategy to step up to supreme ascension had disintegrated into a downward, demonic descent to death.

Judas had heard it said by others that just before a person dies, his life flashes before his eyes. Just before the moment of his own tor-tured demise, he found it was true . . .

He'd grown up in a little town in Judea called Kerioth not far from the capital of Jerusalem. The name his father, Simon, had given him was common, one of the two most often conferred on boy children. As with so many generations throughout history, names meant a blend of identification and expectation for those who carried them.

"Jesus" and "Judas"—the two most popular names of the day represented the longings and distinctiveness of their people. "Jesus" . . . "Yeshua," as they pronounced it, meant "salvation." It alluded to their national longing for their Messiah to come, the Deliverer who would finally set them free from all oppression and tyranny. The occupation of the hated Romans had only intensified that yearning in their generation. "Judas," or its derivatives, such as "Judah," meant "praise" and tied them to their very name as a nation—Judea. They were to be the unique people among all the tribes and tongues of the earth specially designated to represent Yahweh and reveal His glory to all nations. That distinctive was a cause for great pride and preservation. They were God's chosen to carry on His traditions and revelations!

Living so close to Jerusalem where the Temple stood as the national center of religious passion, and the Fortress of Antonia located near it represented Rome's political oppression, had a striking and ongoing effect on a young boy growing into manhood. The line between loyalty to God and duty to country blurred until they were indiscernible. Outward shows of religious piety were allowed, but overt political protests were violently and quickly smashed by Roman steel with deadly efficiency.

Covert bands of men fueled by religious zeal and angry patriotism formed to fight the hated occupiers through stealth and subversion. They were called Zealots. One of the most deadly groups became known as the Sicarii because of their preference for sudden slashing strikes with sharp steel; what they couldn't shout to a soldier's face in public they did with a thrust of a knife from the shadows.

Judas found himself part of a movement whose ends justified any means. Verbally they proclaimed the values of faith, freedom, family, country. But in reality, whatever was deemed expedient made embracing those values expendable. Each small victory was celebrated; but when Judas looked at the bigger picture, he realized they were making pitiful progress. They were a pariah to the general public and "public enemy number one" to the Romans.

Judas had always been a calculating man. Short of stature, he was always trying to project a taller profile to those around him. People often remarked that there appeared to be a lot going on behind those sharp, dark eyes of his—as if he were always trying to see things from a bunch of different angles and figure out which angle worked best for him.

He moved to Jerusalem where his attention to details and love of money led him to work in the Temple treasury—the people's bank. People had to pay a fee to exchange money with Roman images on it—designated unclean because it was desecrated by a Gentile affiliation—to the Temple currency developed by the religious leaders with the approved symbols on them. The symbols and the obscene profits were all that mattered to the priests running the religious machine; any spiritual resemblance was just the façade for the vast empire they ruled. Judas watched, listened and learned, and skimmed a share for his own profit that he felt appropriate but not discernible. Why not? It fit the reality of that culture: position triumphed over humble piety, power trumped humility, politics tainted any real spirituality. As much as the High Priests, the ruling council called the Sanhedrin, the Sadducees and Pharisees and priests that made up the strata of religious leaders denounced Rome's occupation with righteous indignation to the common folks that filled the Temple Courts. Behind the scenes they cut deals that would allow them to maintain their power and income. The Temple that stood shining in the sunlight covered an ugly underbelly of hypocrisy and greed.

Judas was living in two worlds—the secret life of a Sicarrii Zealot and the outward life of a public servant working in God's Temple. He learned how to get what he wanted in both environments, developing the art of always being where important people and decisions were being made and influencing things to his benefit with a suggestion or observation inserted at a tactical moment yet without somehow being obvious or very visible. He enjoyed the ability to manipulate people into doing his bidding while all the time they thought they were acting on their own ideas.

Both worlds nourished his underlying motivations of greed and ambition. A small man unnoticed by most, Judas harbored ambitions and greed far bigger than anyone realized. Neither world, he realized, would get him to his final destination. Both "patriots" and "priests" were contaminated by priorities too personal and petty to accomplish the bigger picture, which was a nation purged from outside oppression and living out its intended destiny with Judas himself well situ-

ated in a position of power, wealth and security. That unseen motivation was fueled by his own ambition; and though he did not recognize it, increasingly it was fed by dark, unseen spiritual influences.

There had to be something else . . . no, *someone* else who could
bring together all the competing agendas and groups, someone who
could unite and galvanize the people into an unstoppable conquering force. *That* was what the Messiah was for. Judas's messianic vision
focused on someone that activated political liberation instead of personal salvation. People longed for and talked about the coming Messiah. Occasionally someone would rise to capture people's attention
with his rhetoric or claims of supernatural help; but like the falling
stars Judas often saw in the night skies above their land, the messianic hope appeared brilliantly but briefly and quickly flamed out
into obscurity.

One day, as he listened to the gossip around the Temple, his ears
perked up as a new name started creating a buzz of interest. At first he
dismissed what he was hearing . . . the man was from Galilee, considered by more sophisticated Jerusalemites as lower class, backwoods
and definitely unappealing. The thought of a national hero arising
from Galilean "Hicksville" didn't make any sense. Still, stories continued to circulate about a carpenter from Nazareth, and Judas' finely
tuned radar determined that a trip north might not be a bad idea.

When he got there he was impressed in spite of himself. It wasn't
hard to locate Jesus of Nazareth. Both the local synagogue leaders
and nearly everyone else was aware of where Jesus was and what He
was doing. He had appeared almost out of nowhere, known only as
a well-regarded, unassuming man running his father's carpentry
business until recently. For no apparent reason, He had suddenly
stepped into a place of people's attention. Stories about Him turning
water into wine at a wedding, and His teaching that captivated people's attention far more than any of the local preachers began to dominate conversations at common gathering places. So Judas found the
Nazarene's latest whereabouts and joined the crowd that had gathered to see what He'd do next.

He didn't disappoint. There was nothing showy or spectacular
about Jesus—He looked ordinary enough and made no moves to call
attention to Himself. Yet as Judas observed with cynical, objective,

appraising eyes, everything Jesus did was extraordinary—what He did, what He said, how people responded to Him. This Jesus was a magnet, appealing to people's deepest needs and longings in a way that Judas had never seen before. Not only did He appeal to them, but He also met them!

Judas had seen religious hucksters making big claims as a prelude to asking for even bigger offerings. People's temporary emotional highs, supposedly representing physical healing or spiritual deliverance so artfully crafted by the spiritual showmen quickly dissipated after the show was done. Judas had seen some of the best their region had to offer around Jerusalem. But this . . . it was as if He deliberately tried *not* to call attention to Himself, and He didn't ask for money! This one was different.

Almost before he realized it, the man who had started on the edges of the crowd as an observer found himself drawn closer to learn more about this Jesus. He began to join the smaller groups of people that followed Jesus to more private settings after the more public events had concluded. Occasionally he asked a question in his typically indirect way to probe more into the Nazarene's real identity and agenda. Jesus always turned his way, looking him in the eye, and answered his questions directly in a way that addressed the issue while raising even more questions in Judas's mind at the same time.

Mostly Judas listened, watched, wondered. Could it be that the one person he'd been looking for that could fulfill his messianic expectations was here in the person of Jesus of Nazareth? He wasn't convinced, but the fact that so many other people seemed to be made a big impression on him. Judas calculated what his involvement with the Galilean might be . . .

It was only a matter of days before his opportunity came. Jesus climbed up one of the high spots of the region one night, saying He needed to spend some time with His Father. He'd stayed there all night, and when He came back down the next morning, He told the group waiting for Him that He wanted some of them to come with Him as His disciples. This would become His inner circle . . . the ones who would get to know the real man . . . the real story . . . the real agenda. If this Jesus was a realistic possibility to meet Judas's expectations, this was the group to belong to. Judas stepped closer, consciously making himself more visible.

Jesus began to go to specific men, one at a time. He would look them in the eye, put His hand on their shoulder and make His invitation to this level of discipleship very personal. Peter; James and John (brothers He nicknamed "Sons of Thunder," most likely for their famous tempers), Andrew, Peter's quiet brother. These were all fishermen from up Capernaum way. The invitations continued. Philip . . . Bartholomew . . . Matthew, a local tax collector that Judas had learned was a cousin of Jesus . . . James the son of Alphaeus . . . Thaddeus . . . Simon, who Judas knew about from his network of fellow Zealots—all were from Jesus' region of the country. To make the normal group of 12, Jesus would have to pick one more . . .

Jesus paused, looking thoughtfully around the group. Many eager, expectant faces returned His gaze, silently pleading for Him to invite them. Then, as if coming to a conclusion, He stepped over to Judas and invited him. "Judas, would you join me?" He asked, looking intently into his eyes. With a simple "Yes," Judas was in.

From the very beginning Judas had felt like an outsider. He was the only one not from Galilee, and he had a hard time keeping his natural prejudice against people from that region in check. He stayed a bit detached, always with the group, trying to act as if he was joining in, yet holding himself back. He continued to watch and evaluate to see how his expectations were lining up with the reality of being part of Jesus' team.

The crowds continued to grow. People began to support the itinerant carpenter-teacher to assist His ministry or to give out of sheer gratitude after Jesus had met their need or a loved one's need. Judas mentioned to Jesus that he had a background of working with money, so Jesus appointed him the group's financial manager. He kept careful track of income and even more careful oversight of the outflow of the money. He kept all the money right with him in a money belt he wrapped securely around him. It provided security for a man whose identity was so closely tied to money. As he always had done, he quietly paid himself a small percentage from the ministry account for his services.

Jesus never seemed to pay a lot of attention to the financial side of things, saying often that they would put God's kingdom first, His

Father would make sure that all their needs were met. They always had more than they needed, and Jesus regularly directed Judas to give generously to people with requests for help. Judas obeyed reluctantly, hating every time he had to give their money to people he felt didn't deserve it. No one seemed to notice, because Judas was a master at hiding his true feelings and intentions. Yet, Jesus would often give Judas a look of encouragement and a knowing warning when He saw those dark eyes cloud over with frustration after yet another directive to share liberally.

Following Jesus was both exhilarating and troubling to Judas. All the components of making Jesus a singular, galvanizing leader to lead the nation appeared to be coming into place—the rising groundswell of popularity, the blend of religious teaching and extraordinary results, the hints from well-placed sources that people's support of Jesus could be leveraged strategically when the right time came. Judas kept his contacts with the Zealots and the religious leaders active. At the right time . . .

What troubled Judas was that Jesus seemed oblivious to the opportunities to advance such an agenda. He called people to commitment, to follow God and serve others in love and holiness instead of fulfilling a personal or political agenda. He offered a life of freedom and joyful abundance regardless of external circumstances. Jesus was much too spiritual for Judas' liking; a more pragmatic approach was needed to make the most of these open doors. He'd hinted at this numerous times, but Jesus would just give him a knowing look, shake His head and turn it into another teachable moment designed for the heart. Jesus seemed impervious to Judas's attempts to "help him along." There was no manipulating Him.

Three years had gone by and Judas was getting increasingly impatient and irritated. They'd traveled all over the region, only occasionally getting to Jerusalem where the real action was. Judas had been unable to crack the innermost circle of three made up of Peter, James and John. Seeds of jealousy he'd allowed to take root in his heart sprouted and grew, watered by his own broodings and ambitions. The dark whispers from the shadows became more insistent and easier to listen to.

Then something shifted. They all felt it, and Jesus told them plainly one night. It was time to go to Jerusalem. For a brief moment, a surge of excitement rose within Judas. Perhaps this was the moment he'd been waiting for! It would be during Passover. The city would swell with multitudes of pilgrims in town for the religious festival; some estimated the population of Jerusalem would grow to two and a half times its normal size. If there was ever a time to seize the moment, this would be it!

Then Jesus described a scenario that absolutely made no sense at all. He would be betrayed, He said. He would suffer at the hands of the religious leaders—the very ones who were supposed to recognize and rise to confirm the Messiah's plans for victory. He said He'd die . . . and then rise again in three days. From one perspective, this all fit perfectly into everything Jesus had been teaching about and living for. It was His mission. From Judas's perspective, it was the exact opposite of his expectations. *What was he going to do now?*

As they walked toward Jerusalem, Judas calculated. If Jesus was truly headed toward a confrontation with the Romans and the Jewish religious leaders that ended in His death, then being identified with Jesus could easily mean his own death too. With Jesus' death would come the end of His ministry and the end of the money Judas had managed and profited from. Judas wondered if there was a way to distance himself from Jesus, ingratiate himself with people of influence and make some money at the same time.

Or . . . with the right assistance, perhaps Jesus could be convinced to truly take His place as the political and religious king of the nation. If He was the Messiah, wouldn't this be the right time to ascend to power?! Could Judas somehow make all these options work for his benefit? The small man brooded, calculated . . . and the whispers from the dark contributed to his inner conversation.

They arrived in Jerusalem on Sunday to vast cheering throngs of people . . . a welcome fit for a king! Judas reveled in the adulation afforded him by being associated with Jesus. This was going in the right direction!

Then things went in the opposite track. The next day, Jesus threw the Temple area into an uproar, upsetting the tables and neatly piled Temple currency into a chaotic blur of rolling coins, and setting free the sacrificial animals for sale that began running and flying in all directions. "This is My Father's house . . . a house of prayer! How dare you turn it into a den of thieves!" He'd roared, His holy anger thrilling and magnificent to watch. People tired of being fleeced by the religious establishment for the privilege of worshiping God stood up and cheered. The money changers, temple workers and priests shook their fists in protest and slunk into the background. Judas knew some of them, and the looks he saw on their faces made him suddenly feel hollow and almost ashamed. Jesus followed that intervention with sharp confrontations with the religious leaders, calling out Sadducees and Pharisees alike by exposing the sins they'd hid so nicely under a religious veneer. Any chance of getting their support was now seemingly obliterated.

Later that night, Judas excused himself from the rest, saying he had errands to run to help their group make Passover preparations. Instead, he met with some of his Temple contacts and found out that Caiaphas the high priest had convened a meeting to deal with the Jesus situation once and for all. He had declared that it was better for one man to die than for their whole way of life to be lost. But they decided to find a way to arrest and get rid of Jesus away from the adoring crowds. This had to be done deliberately, discreetly and delicately.

When Judas heard that, something inside him trembled. This thing was coming to a head. His calculating mind raced faster. Was there still a way to rescue this situation? He felt pulled in so many directions. He wanted Jesus to live up to his expectations. After all, the Nazarene had always been good to him. His ambitions still hoped for Jesus to become king and Judas to benefit from that association. He wanted to protect himself in case the plans of the chief priests continued toward getting rid of Jesus. He didn't want any arrest warrant for Jesus and His followers to have his name on it. His greed still wanted to find an angle to make the situation profitable. The whispers from the darkness fed the ambition and greed with their own suggestions, and his confusion grew.

Still, he hoped that somehow Jesus would find His way back to the right messianic path. When they ate an evening meal on Wednesday night, at the home of Simon, in Bethany, things finally reached the breaking point. A woman came and broke a fine alabaster jar of very expensive perfume, pouring it first on Jesus' head and then anointing His feet. The beautiful fragrance of the perfume and this act of love filled the room, but all Judas could see was a year's wages wasted. He'd protested under the guise of saying the money could have been used for the poor; but when Jesus rebuked him and said that she was preparing His body in advance for His death and burial, Judas knew that if anything was to happen to force Jesus' hand in the direction Judas wanted Him to go, he'd have to make it happen himself. Something beyond his ambitions compelled him.

Judas left on another "errand" and this time gained an audience with Caiaphas and his inner circle of advisors. They stood for a moment appraising each other—Caiaphas and Judas both shrewd manipulators trying to figure out how to gain the upper hand. "What will you give me to hand over Jesus of Nazareth to you?" Judas said. Sudden interest and a gleam of triumph showed in Caiaphas's eyes. This was exactly what he'd been hoping for—someone on the inside of Jesus' organization who could orchestrate the right scenario for His arrest! Speaking deliberately to try to hide his delight, Caiaphas questioned the little man to make sure he could deliver. He could.

They set the price at 30 pieces of silver—the price of a slave—with a hint that this was just the first installment if things went as Judas promised. They shook hands on the deal, each one's palm feeling greasy to the other, each feeling they had gotten the best part of the deal.

Caiaphas was now indebted to Judas. No matter which way the situation went, he could take the side that best protected him. Caiaphas cared nothing for Judas . . . the one piece of his plan he'd needed had neatly fallen into place.

Judas began to look for the right time . . .

The next day was filled with people, activity and Passover preparations. Nothing presented itself, and Judas pondered what to do. Where was a good place that was out of the way, easy to access under the cover of darkness and offered escape routes if he needed one? Suddenly he realized the right place. The garden at Gethsemane where Jesus often took them to pray in the evenings . . . that would be just right!

Late afternoon shadows were lengthening across Jerusalem, but no one could see that the shadows of darkness were getting stronger in Judas too. Always before he'd been able to squelch the whispers when he wanted to; but with his decision to hand Jesus over, the voices had gained more power. They crowded in on him, pressuring him, gaining more and more control.

The Jesus team had gathered in an upper room that Jesus had arranged to be prepared for the Passover meal. It was a sacred remembrance of their history, a tradition that generations had followed. They all knew the celebration ritual by heart. Entering the room, Jesus had quietly asked Judas to take the place to His left when they reclined at the low table—the place reserved for the honored guest. The host could lean his head back close to the person in that position and share privately. It was a position anyone invited to a meal would covet, and Jesus was inviting him to take that place! Judas nodded, confused. What was this supposed to mean? Did Jesus somehow know what he had done? Why should he get this honor?

They began the meal, enjoying the fellowship and food as part of the time-honored tradition. Jesus seemed unusually pensive, letting the conversation flow around Him as the others recapped their day. Judas glanced over at Him several times, wondering . . .

Then Jesus looked up and the room fell silent as the Twelve sensed He was about to share something important. For a long moment the room was quiet, but tension hung thickly in the air. Suddenly they were going off the familiar script. Looking around the table at each one, Jesus said slowly, "One of you is going to betray me."

The shock was immediate and visceral. What?! *One of them?* They all began to protest at once, declaring their loyalty and asking who the traitor could be. Judas said nothing, quivering inside. One word from Jesus and he'd be exposed and the other 11 men would make sure he never left that room alive.

John, reclining at Jesus' right, leaned his head back and whispered something to Jesus. Jesus whispered something back too low for Judas to hear. John looked over at Peter at the end of the table and made the slightest nod of his head in Judas's direction. Jesus lifted His hand palm outward in a "stop" motion to Peter. Realizing that he hadn't said anything yet, Judas spoke, his voice sounding unnatural from the strain, but he managed to get the words out. "Surely not I, Rabbi?" Not Lord. Not Master. Just Rabbi. Teacher.

Then Jesus took a piece of bread from His plate, dipped it into the bowl of sauce in front of him and turned to extend it to Judas.

The simple gesture had incredible significance. When the host took from his own plate and offered it to one of the guests like that, it was a supreme indication of favor and friendship—an invitation to intimacy.

As Jesus held the bread toward Judas, their eyes met and the wordless conversation forever cemented Judas's destiny.

Jesus knew.

Suddenly it was clear to Judas that Jesus knew His betrayer. Yet, with His extended hand was the offer of the bread of friendship and one last chance to turn back from his betrayal. Here it was, the final choice: friendship and commitment to discipleship on Jesus' terms, or a forced relationship where Jesus had to meet Judas's expectations on his terms.

Judas chose. If he was going to be identified with Jesus, it would be on Judas's terms. He'd force the Nazarene's hand, if He truly was the Messiah, to do it according to Judas's plan.

He leaned forward, smiling, and ate the bread from Jesus' hand.

From the look in Jesus' eyes, Judas could tell He understood the choice Judas had made. Speaking so low it was hard for the others to hear, Jesus looked steadily into Judas's eyes and said, "Do what you're going to do, and do it quickly."

A cold chill made Judas shudder involuntarily, and in that instant the door he'd closed to Jesus opened another to the darkness . . . and the darkness came rushing in. Suddenly Judas was dimly aware that he was under the control of another. The voices seemed to all clamor at once and then stop as if silenced. One voice, darker than any he'd ever heard, now directed him. It was time to go.

Rising to his feet without another word, Judas wrapped his garment around him and left the room, leaving behind the puzzled gazes of the other disciples and the lingering image of the face of Jesus. He stepped out into the darkness of chosen sin and satanic possession.

From then on Judas felt as if he was operating at another person's coercion. He found his way back to the Temple where Caiaphas waited. Money was counted into Judas's hands. He put the money into his belt, tying it tightly about him. Somehow it felt tighter than before—like it was squeezing him, slowly suffocating him. He was dully surprised when he saw the mob they'd assembled to arrest Jesus. There were dozens of fully armed Roman soldiers, Temple guards with their uniforms and weapons, other Temple workers who'd grabbed the nearest thing they could find as a weapon, priests with small reputations and big ambitions who wanted to get in on the action. Hundreds had assembled armed to the teeth to arrest the most peaceful man he'd ever met!

The dark one forced him forward under the full Passover moon, the moonlight and flickering illumination of torches and lanterns casting eerie shadows as they went. The shadows seemed alive, grasping for him, taunting him. The dark pressure inside compelled him on.

They were in the Garden now and Judas turned to the soldiers closest to him. "Remember, the one I greet with a kiss is the one. That will be the signal." They continued on, the rumble of voices seen and unseen growing in his mind.

In an open clearing in the midst of the olive trees, one man stood alone, waiting for them. When Judas saw Him, the dark one inside him seemed to rise with an ugly, unearthly pleasure. The betrayer was being used by another betrayer.

Judas stepped forward, his face smiling with an unnatural greeting. His face felt frozen, his movements wooden. Walking up to Jesus, he stopped and stood a step away, breathing heavily. Jesus looked at him and said softly, "Friend, do what you've come for." There was a pause. Judas could feel his heart beating. Then that dark unseen hand pulled him forward and Judas heard his voice as if someone else was using it. "Greetings, Rabbi!" One last step. Taking Jesus by the shoulders as a friend would greet a friend, Judas kissed him once . . . twice . . . and again as if for emphasis. Jesus looked down at him and Judas felt like Jesus was reaching past the dark presence that possessed him to the real person submerged under the spiritual domination. "Judas . . ." Jesus' voice was overruling all the other voices and touching his heart one last time, "you betray the Son of Man with a kiss?"

Judas stepped to the side. He'd done his part. Now Jesus was supposed to do His. All He had to do was take control like He had done so many times before.

Jesus stood tall and strong in the moonlight. "Who is it you are looking for?" He asked the crowd loud enough so that everyone could hear.

Someone cleared his throat. "Jesus, the Nazarene." It was hundreds against one, but the voice sounded a bit fearful. They'd all heard of what the Nazarene could do; and if He turned His power loose on them—

"I AM!" Jesus' ringing response reverberated with divine power, and the force of His words pushed them to the ground. His response was the same response Moses got at the burning bush when he asked Yahweh's identity. They cringed, expecting divine wrath to swallow them up.

Nothing happened. Jesus still stood unwavering in the moonlight, waiting for them. Again the question came. "Who are you looking for?" Another voice answered, a bit bolder this time.

"Jesus of Nazareth."

"I told you, I am He. So if you are looking for me, then let the rest of these men go."

A cry came from behind Jesus, and Peter came out of the shadows, swinging and slashing with a short sword. A man fell to Judas's right, crying out in pain. The sound of dozens of swords sliding from their scabbards filled the air. The situation was starting to careen into deadly chaos.

Jesus took control. He knelt and healed the man, reattaching the man's severed ear. Peter and the disciples ran. Judas stood there frozen in place. Tentatively, then as one man, the mob surged forward and surrounded Jesus. Rough hands grabbed Him and tied His hands behind His back, forcing His thumbs up into His shoulders. Other hands formed fists and let out their pent-up anxiety and anger as they pummeled Jesus' face and body. Unseen voices cackled with glee as they saw His pain.

Then the mob was gone with their prey. Judas was forgotten. He stood alone. The evil one that had been using him left. His purpose was done. The darkness wouldn't need him anymore.

For a long moment Judas stood there blinking, trying to comprehend what had just happened. Everything had gone according to his plan. Nothing was going according to plan. Slowly it dawned on him that he'd been played, in a much bigger game, and on more levels than he could understand.

Dumbly, he stumbled back the way he'd come, following the last vestiges of light from the departing mob. When he arrived at the courtyard of Caiaphas's home, it was filled with the remnant of the arrestors and a growing number of others who'd heard the news and wanted to gawk at unfolding events. For the middle of the night, the place was alive with laughter and anticipation. Those who recognized Judas congratulated him on his achievement. He'd delivered the one man they'd all wanted, making him their hero. Judas didn't feel like one.

What now? Maybe Jesus would still exert Himself. Judas waited along with the others while the night wore on, hoping to hear some word of what was happening. Fear began to grow as he realized that his calculations had gone entirely wrong and others' calculations—the ones who had used him—completely right. Word started circulating in whispers around him . . . they'd declared a death sentence on Jesus. He'd go to Pilate in the morning. With that news Judas knew Jesus' execution was certain. He heard Jesus' voice again: "Judas, you betray the Son of Man with a kiss?" A verse from Psalm 41 surfaced in his mind, *"Even my friend in whom I trusted, one who ate my bread, has lifted up his heel against me."* It was the betrayer's verse.

Suddenly he was gripped with a deep sense of remorse. He had betrayed an innocent man. This wasn't justice; it was sacrilege! It wasn't supposed to end like this. Wait . . . maybe there was one last move to try to undo the chain of events he'd willingly but uncomprehendingly instigated. The law said that if he gave back the money, the deal he'd made with the High Priest would be nullified. They'd have to let Jesus go. Surely they'd honor their own law . . .

He felt the darkness closing in again—as if now released, the voices came upon him with a vengeance—protesting, pushing, pounding at his mind, clawing at his spirit. Although he could see nothing, he was in sudden physical pain from the violence. Willing himself against the pressure, he walked in a weaving, almost careening, path to the Temple, where he'd been paid by the priests. The first streaks of dawn were showing in the east.

He staggered through the doorway, gasping with the effort. He was drenched with sweat, his eyes bulging, lips quivering.

The priests on duty turned to see a disheveled heap of a man in front of them, and it made them uneasy just to look at them. With visible effort, he spoke, trying to restrain the madness around him.

"I have sinned."

They smiled cynically at him, saying nothing. Hadn't he just been here hours earlier, a self-assured, conniving traitor?

"I have sinned," Judas said again. "I've betrayed innocent blood . . . an innocent man." The unspoken words were, "I want to call the whole thing off."

They laughed at him. "What do we care? That's your problem."

What?! These were priests, representatives of God. He'd just confessed sin. They were supposed to find a way for him to be forgiven, to make things right. They'd shut the door of restoration in his face. If there was no hope from them, then there was no hope.

No hope.

Now the voices reached shrieking intensity, and he groaned in agony at their onslaught. To the priests, it sounded like a trapped animal.

Reaching under his cloak, he tore off his money belt and counted out 30 silver coins with trembling hands. They had to take the money back . . . they had to take the money back!

With a snarl he threw the money at them, the ringing sounds of silver on stone loud in the room. Then he was gone.

He never heard what the priests said next, and if he had it would have only compounded his horror. They had decided that since this was blood money, they couldn't use it for Temple purposes. So they'd buy a "field of blood" as burial ground for those who were alienated from their own cemeteries by uncleanness—a place they called "the potter's field." Unknowingly, they'd fulfilled another prophecy spoken by Jeremiah and recorded in Zechariah 11:12-13: *Give me my wages. . . . So they counted out for my wages thirty pieces of silver. And the LORD said to me, 'Throw it to the potters'—this magnificent sum at which they valued me! So I took the thirty coins and threw them to the potters in the Temple of the LORD.* Over the generations that parcel had become a place of sacrifices to demons, of human slaughter and suffering and demonic gloom. Some thought it was the doorway to hell.

Judas was on his way there now. He had no idea where he was going, but the voices did. They slashed and poked and prodded and pushed him as he ran headlong through the narrow streets, faster than his legs could carry him at times. Each time he fell, the voices clawed at him until he got up and lurched ahead again. They pushed him along until he reached the gate on the road that led to Bethlehem, now swollen with incoming pilgrims. Judas swam against the incoming tide of people, legs churning and arms thrashing, leaving a wake of people staring in bewilderment after him.

Outside the gate, the forces pushed him along a little path clinging to the bottom of the wall that hung over the Valley of Hinnom. The path hung on the edge of the sheer rock face. Far below were the sharp, jagged remnants of stone from the wall's construction and the open arms of demonic destruction. The field he'd just purchased with his blood money was down in the valley below him. He'd sold them his soul and now he was going to pay. The soil that had received the blood of countless sacrifices to Satan was about to receive his.

A tree hung over the edge. Judas stopped, realizing he was still holding his money belt in his hand. That belt had represented his identity and security . . . it had been his life. Now it was going to cause his death.

He pushed on the trunk of the little tree and it moved only slightly. Trembling, he climbed out on the trunk and leaned on a branch. It gave way a little more. The voices were so loud now that he couldn't hear anything else. They snarled, taunted, cajoled, jeered, accused . . .

No hope . . . no hope . . . no hope . . . no hope . . . no hope . . .

He tied one end of his money belt to the limb; the other end he wrapped around his neck.

No hope . . . no hope . . . no hope . . . no hope . . . no hope.

It wasn't supposed to end like this.

He whimpered at the thought of what was coming, but the voices kept pushing. Leaning forward, he let go. His body fell downward, suddenly stopping with a jerk as the belt stretched taunt. For a moment he swung back and forth as life was squeezed out of him.

Then the branch snapped, and he fell headlong, face-first, to the sharp rocks below that looked like the bared teeth of a gaping mouth. With a sickening sound his guts splattered across the stones, and the soil lapped up his spilt blood.

The betrayer had been betrayed . . .

by his own ambitions and expectations and manipulations . . .

by satanic forces that turned his calculations and decisions back on him . . .

by trying to force God to submit to his own plans.

And as with everyone who insists on his way over God's, his choices killed him.

Judas was dead before the Messiah who would give His life for betrayers like him.

BEYOND THE STORY
To Help You Think, Pray, Share and Do

1. How did the people and experiences of your growing-up years affect your spiritual attitudes?

2. Judas's downfall began when he tried to use religion for his own ends. How might you relate to that? How does this serve as a warning for you?

3. When we resist what Jesus has to say, we open ourselves up to other voices. Satan is a master at suggesting what sounds reasonable but is really deception. What are some ways you can discern the source of what you "hear"?

4. What we worship will ultimately take us down when we don't choose to trust Christ with our whole heart. Jesus said you can't trust both God and money, because you'll wind up loving one and hating the other. Judas is a tragic example of this truth. Are there any divided loyalties in your life . . . any rivals to the complete Lordship of Jesus? What might you need to surrender so that you belong to Jesus alone?

6

A Reluctant Judge

(Pontius Pilate)

John 18:28–19:16

The first glow of yellow on the horizon was turning the night's inky darkness into the gray of dawn.

Surrounded by the cold stone pillars and walls of his palace, Pontius Pilate shivered as he waited, warming his hands over a charcoal fire. He cursed inwardly at having to get up so early, and cursed the reason he was awaiting his visitors.

He was not anxious for the day's events to begin. Soon, he was informed, a man would be brought before him to judge and sentence. The religious leaders of Jerusalem, in reality more politically than spiritually motivated, had been in contact with Pilate's people about a deal. The prisoner they were bringing was a threat to their empire and, they reminded Pilate's underlings, a threat to Rome's as well. That insinuation had made Pilate laugh out loud. There had been numerous attempts over the years to unseat Rome's rule in this little province. Jesus of Nazareth seemed among the most unlikely of candidates to try it again. Still, Pilate knew this day would be coming.

For months reports had been getting back to him about the person he would judge today. From all the information he had been able to gather, Jesus of Nazareth was not a political climber, a military insurrectionist or a publicity seeker. He was a carpenter in his early thirties, unmarried and of lower economic class from a little town to the north called Nazareth. No one around Jerusalem had even heard of Jesus until he had left his home and started speaking in the villages around Nazareth about three years ago.

His speaking had at first attracted the attention of the more religiously inclined, but soon people came to realize there was more to

Jesus than just religious talk. Reports of supernatural occurrences began to get back to Pilate. Wherever Jesus of Nazareth went, miracles were sure to follow. Skeptical soldiers Pilate had sent to be firsthand witnesses recounted incidents that still left them wide-eyed in wonder. Blind people gained their sight. Deaf people's ears were opened to sound. Crippled people danced on restored limbs. Wild-eyed people possessed by who knew what instantaneously returned to sanity. Diseased people regained their health. There were even stories of dead people resurrected to life. At first Pilate had discounted the stories, but as time and the stories of miracles continued to accumulate, he couldn't ignore this Jesus anymore. Vast crowds of people went to hear Him wherever He went. His name seemed to be on everyone's lips. The simple carpenter from Nazareth became the most controversial figure in the nation.

His popularity was a paradox. Jesus had never advocated rebellion against Rome. His organization seemed to consist of only a dozen men and a few women. He had made no attempt to gain power of any kind. In fact, Pilate had heard that on more than one occasion Jesus had resisted attempts by the masses to thrust Him into political prominence.

His teaching and actions resembled those of a servant more than a celebrity. Still, Pilate was also aware that Annas and Caiaphas, the leaders of Jerusalem's religious and financial empire, increasingly viewed Jesus as a threat. He was well aware of their desire to get rid of Him. They saw Him as a rival. Others, however, lauded Him as a savior. Some were calling Him a king. Others didn't know what to think of Him, but everyone had heard of Jesus of Nazareth.

Last night, even Pilate's wife, Claudia, had told him how she would sometimes watch the crowds and the man called Jesus from her litter as she was being carried to various places by their servants. She even repeated some of the things she'd heard Jesus teach, and in her retelling, Pilate could sense she had been deeply moved by what she'd heard. She was too emotional for his tastes most of the time, but her female intuitive discernment was usually right when his male logic was off the mark. He was still troubled by her words: "This Jesus is unlike anyone I've ever seen or heard about. Be careful. Maybe he really is a god in the form of a man." She had been reflective in that way she was when she was right on target with her assessments of people or situations. Pilate shook his head at the memory and drew his robe more closely around him.

Now they were bringing this Jesus of Nazareth to him.

Moodily, Pilate reflected on his own position. He had been sent to be the chief administrator and governor over the Roman province of Palestine. Pilate had risen to the top by the usual means. He was a veteran soldier and had married Caesar's granddaughter. Stepping around, over and usually on top of all opponents, he had climbed the ladder until the appointment to Palestine came. The dusty little country was not necessarily a desirable assignment, but being a governor had a certain amount of prestige and power he enjoyed. One had to start somewhere if he wanted to climb the ladder of success back to a place of honor in Rome. Palestine was his somewhere.

The people he governed were a strange lot. The little country had a long history of religious and civil unrest. They were for the most part very religious, sometimes to the point of a fanaticism he didn't understand. Yet, in spite of their expressed spiritual convictions, he had seen their own susceptibility to greed and power corrupt them like any other people. Their religion had a great deal of outward form and ritual, but apparently little inward power to change the motivations of the heart.

Pilate had a soldier's contempt for religion. When younger he had tried appeasing the gods in hopes that it would further his career. Not seeing the results he wanted soon enough, he had given up on religion. He had seen plenty of religion in his military travels—idols and ceaseless prayers and fear and suspicion and frustration. He would have none of that!

For him, the motto "might makes right" had worked well. Give him power—a legion of hardened veterans, trusty swords, sharp spears and shiny armor. That was his security! He had done well trusting his fate to himself. No gods could claim credit for his rise to power.

Yes, Pilate mused, *I am truly a self-made man.* His own hard work and shrewd manipulating of opportunities had paid off. He had all a person could want—position, wealth, power, luxury and material prosperity. Yet, smiling grimly to himself, he faced his reality with a sense of irony. In spite of all he had, he remained an empty man. Something had eluded him all his life. There was a void inside that couldn't be filled by his might and fierce Roman pride.

Pilate had it all, but he had no meaning to fill his heart with purpose, to make life worthwhile. A soldier appeared from behind one of the marble pillars informing him the party of priests and the prisoner had arrived.

Pilate's thoughts snapped back to disciplined attention. Wrapping his purple toga around him against the morning chill, he went out into the courtyard. He cursed again at their silly religious rules that made him go out to meet them. They were in the midst of a religious observance that prohibited them from being in the home of a Gentile. Stepping inside his place would render them unclean. He snorted in contempt. He already felt a little dirty about the way this whole incident was being handled.

Morning light had advanced to the point where Pilate could make out the features and expressions of the crowd who faced him.

The group was comprised of religious leaders, dressed in their fine robes, looking haggard from lack of sleep. With them were palace guards holding spears, and hired rabble consisting of local ruffians armed with clubs. They had thrust the prisoner in front of them.

Viewing the crowd, he saw many faces look back at him with ill-concealed intolerance and pious pride. They looked more to Pilate like a pack of snarling animals waiting for a kill than righteous religious people. Pilate then sized up the prisoner and immediately saw it was the only calm face in the seething crowd.

His soldier's eyes noticed that the prisoner carried no weapons.

The prisoner was dressed in a plain, seamless robe, soiled from dirt and spit. His hands were tied behind His back and His face showed evidence of the beating He had already received. One eye was turning an ugly dark blue, and His cheek displayed an angry red spot from repeated blows. Portions of His beard had been pulled out.

Outwardly the man was a pathetic sight.

But Pilate had not risen to his position by viewing outward appearances only. He looked past the clothes to see the man Himself. The face, though bruised, remained calm and was held high.

Pilate had seen many prisoners in his time—wild-eyed revolutionaries who struggled and cursed the hated Romans; common thieves, repentant for their crimes only because they had been caught. Pilate had sentenced two thieves to death only yesterday.

He had even seen other religious prisoners on assorted charges eagerly willing to turn over a new spiritual leaf in exchange for freedom.

Yet, this man was like none of them. There was something different about him. He had a bearing that made Pilate sense in an odd way that Jesus was more in control of the situation than he was. There was a depth in those eyes that attracted Pilate. He himself had been in the presence of royalty many times, and strangely, in the presence of this man he felt that he was in the presence of royalty once again.

Finally, Pilate spoke, "What charges are you bringing against this man?"

The reply was insolent and brusque. "If he were not a criminal," they replied, "we would not have handed him over to you."

Pilate answered in the same tone. Turning to go, he said, "Take him yourselves and judge him by your own law." Deal or no deal, he wasn't going to put up with that kind of obvious disrespect.

A murmur swept through the crowd. The high priest gasped and stepped forward to object. "But we have no right to execute anyone," he complained.

Pilate turned back to them. His eyes narrowed. So that was it! His role was only to give his stamp of approval so they could kill Jesus.

Pilate looked at the prisoner again. Suddenly he had an urge to talk to this man privately. There was more than met the eye here. He'd heard all the stories about Jesus, but this was the first time the two had met personally. He needed to find out more about this man for himself.

He motioned brusquely to the soldiers and had Him brought inside.

Once inside, Pilate viewed the prisoner. In spite of himself, he was impressed with the calmness he saw in Jesus, who stood without speaking, looking at the man in front of Him. This was the one that some people were calling the King of the Jews.

"Are you King of the Jews?"

Pilate's question came out so softly it surprised him. He really wanted to know!

Jesus' eyes searched Pilate, and He smiled faintly.

"Is it your own idea, or did others talk to you about me?"

The direct response to his own query startled the Roman. Jesus had forced him to qualify his statement. Did he really want to know personally if Jesus was who he claimed to be, or was he only curious about the issues of Roman law? For the first time Pilate felt like the one being searched for answers.

"Do you think I am a Jew?" Pilate replied, a bit irritated at feeling like he was not in control of the conversation. "It was your people and your chief priests who handed you over to me. What have you done? Are you seeking to overthrow Rome with a kingdom of your own?"

All Jesus had to do was deny the charges and Pilate could set Him free. But Jesus answered Pilate's question directly.

"My kingdom is not of this world. If it were, my servants would fight to prevent my arrest by the Jews. But now my kingdom is from another place."

Jesus looked past the armor and fine clothes and hardened exterior of the Roman and saw into his heart. He was getting to Pilate's real need—not of a kingdom of might but a King who could bring meaning to his life!

"You are a king, then!" said Pilate. As improbable as is sounded, the words of Jesus rang true.

Jesus answered, and now it was He who spoke as Son of God to a searching man. "You are right in saying I am a king. In fact, for this reason I was born, and for this cause I came into the world, to testify to the truth. Everyone on the side of truth listens to me."

Whose side was *he* on? The question came instinctively, automatically to Pilate. He'd always confessed to being on the side of Rome. In reality he had always been on his own side. Now Jesus was making him choose from a new point of view. He had always come down on the side of "might made right." But was might always right? The man in front of him was in a position of no earthly power, but Pilate knew what Jesus was saying was right . . . and true. Jesus' words brought Pilate to a reality that threatened his Roman presuppositions. Might didn't make right. Truth made right.

Whose side *was* he on?

One thing was now clear to Pilate. There was nothing wrong with Jesus. Let the hypocritical religious rulers make their own choices. He would have no part in this mockery of truth and travesty of justice.

He rose, resolute, and went out to face the crowd. For a moment their murmuring stopped as they saw him appear before them.

"You take him. As for me, I find no basis for a charge against this man."

A roar went up. Caiaphas the high priest stepped forward and shouted, "We have a law, and according to that law He must die, because He claimed to be the Son of God. He's been spreading His lies all over our nation, starting in Galilee . . ." The crowd began to shout their agreement with Caiaphas. Now an unruly mob, they began to howl for blood.

Suddenly Pilate sensed a possible out from this uncomfortable scenario. He didn't like feeling like he was being squeezed between the Jewish leaders here and his superiors in Rome. They'd done this to him before, skillfully mixing Roman politics with their religious prejudices, with Pilate becoming the unwilling puppet for their purposes. Memories surfaced his resentment at being used and outmaneuvered by these troublesome Jews.

He was the sixth governor of this Roman province, and Palestine came with a reputation unlike any other place in the empire. They were difficult to rule with their religion at the root of their rebellion. It rose to the surface at the most unlikely and confusing times. Although his headquarters were near the sea at a city renamed Caesarea after the Roman Emperor Caesar, he would often make trips to Jerusalem on Roman business. His Fortress of Antonia in Jerusalem was in proximity to their Temple area—sacred ground for their worship and selling ground for the religious leaders to accumulate wealth. He'd had his soldiers carry the emblems of the empire into Jerusalem—the Roman eagle attached to the top of a pole, symbol of Caesar as conqueror and king. They attached the eagles of Rome on a wall that overlooked the Temple area. It was designed to be a clear statement about who was truly reigning and in control in Jerusalem.

Instead, it threw the entire region into chaos and a life-or-death standoff. Jewish religious leaders incited huge crowds of people in Caesarea and Jerusalem to demand the removal of what they called graven images, which broke the first of their 10 eternal and immutable commandments from God. Jewish emissaries appeared to him at his headquarters in Caesarea with demands to remove the idolatrous images. For five days he refused to hear them, and yet their stipulations grew louder and more insistent. On the sixth day, he allowed the crowd into his courtyard, surrounded them with sword-wielding soldiers and harshly told them that any further clamoring about this matter would result in sudden death from Roman steel. Instead of backing down, the Jews had laid on the ground and bared their necks, roaring that they'd rather die than violate sacred commandments and allow any rival to their God.

Their response had taken Pilate by surprise. He was not used to seeing people willing to die for the sake of their religion. Faced with the prospect of his headquarters courtyard being colored with blood, and the bloodbath then extending to the ends of his now limited rule, he'd backed down. He hated losing at anything, and that defeat had galled him ever since. The uneasy relationship between Pilate and the Sanhedrin leaders became even more tenuous. Any exchange between him and the Jews was tight with tension.

He'd even tried to do something for their benefit as a gesture of goodwill. He'd determined that Jerusalem needed a better water supply, so he used Roman ingenuity to build them a new aqueduct system. However, he'd used monies from their Temple treasury to pay for the expenses—they were already touchy about too many taxes—and the religious leaders turned on him again. They were experts about stirring up uninformed common folk into slogan-shouting, emotionally crazed mobs. When they did it again, this time Pilate was ready. He sent in soldiers dressed as civilians, and at his signal they turned on the rioters with wooden staves and beat them into submission. Somehow word got back to Rome about the incident and it had strained his relationship with Caesar, to whom he reported directly. Rome did not like reports of ongoing upheavals when Pax Romana was supposed to be the norm. Even in winning, they'd done it to him again. No matter what he did, Annas and Caiaphas would find a way to make him an embarrassing example of Roman arrogance and the object of Jewish hatred.

However, when he heard the word "Galilee," his chance for delicious revenge and political irony came clearly into view. Galilee represented Herod Antipas, a Gentile political appointee with no Jewish blood assigned to rule Jewish rabble "up north" in an area considered to be backwoods and backwards. Herod was resented almost as much as Pilate among Jewish people. Pilate and Herod had sparred over political boundaries and played one-upmanship power games more than once. Herod had well earned his reputation as a conniving, egotistical fox. Their relationship had been sporadic and prickly at best. Then Pilate's soldiers had mistakenly killed some of Herod's subjects and all communication between the two had been cut off.

Now, in the midst of such an inconvenient time, came a win-win opportunity for Pilate. He could get the Nazarene off his hands and extend a gesture of respect to Herod. When reports got back to Rome about how he'd handled the situation involving Jesus, he could say that he'd sought Herod's counsel and turned the case over to him for his decision. In one brilliant stroke he could be free of Jesus, put the problem in Herod's scheming hands and put Annas and Caiaphas into an almost indefensible position. It was almost too good to be true. He sent the prisoner off to Herod's palace with his soldiers to verify the results.

An hour later, his soldiers were back with the prisoner, now dressed in an elegant robe. The centurion reported that Herod had at first received the Nazarene with amusement and then asked Him to validate His reputation with a miracle. When Jesus remained stoic and unyieldingly silent before the bloated buffoon of a ruler, Herod had sent Him back to Pilate with a regal purple robe as his mocking endorsement of Jesus' supposed royalty. Pilate's ploy had utterly failed and now the pressure on him was intensified.

Because only the Roman government could authorize a public execution, Pilate realized once again the decision rested upon him. What would he do with Jesus? He didn't want to have to do anything. He tried again to take away his personal responsibility for the decision. "I will have him flogged and then release him." The crowd only became more frenzied in their anger. Their shouting took on a venomous quality with an ominous unity: "Crucify . . . crucify . . . crucify."

Pilate paled. It was true! No ordinary life hung in the balance here. Pilate was on the verge of making a decision that would affect all eternity.

Quickly he went back inside and spoke to Jesus.

"Where do you come from? Are you really from God?"

Jesus looked him straight in the eyes and said nothing. That decision was to be made by Pilate himself. Jesus was waiting for a decision of faith.

Jesus' words came back to Pilate again: "I came into the world, to testify to the truth. Everyone on the side of truth listens to me."

Pilate now asked the question he had waited so long to hear an answer for: "What is truth?"

Suddenly, standing there, he needed no answer. He was looking at the Answer.

As improbable as it seemed, Pilate's answer to the emptiness of his heart was before him in the person of Jesus of Nazareth.

King of the Jews.

Son of God.

Pilate returned to the entrance to face the mob once more. He was determined that this man be set free. He could not allow this innocent man and the answer to his own quest be killed.

Then it came to him that there was a solution. Surely the people would want Jesus rather than a murderer! He motioned for silence and spoke again.

"I find no basis for a charge against him. But it is your custom for me to release to you one prisoner at the time of Passover. Do you want me to release 'the King of the Jews' or Barabbas, who has taken part in a rebellion?"

At that moment one of Pilate's aides came alongside and whispered to him, placing a note in his hand. He walked off to the side, out of the view of the Jews to see what would cause such an interruption. The note bore Claudia's familiar handwriting. He glanced upward toward their apartment high in a southwestern tower of their fortress. She would be waking up about now and must have heard the commotion below.

He frowned. It was highly unusual for her to insert herself into his work, especially in the midst of an ongoing interrogation. When he read her words, his eyes widened slightly and he felt a lump rise in his throat.

"Have nothing to do with this just man," it read. "I've had a vivid dream about him that troubles me greatly."

Of all the times for her intuition to kick in, why now? He shook his head, trying to clear his mind. Was it possible that she was aware of something that was beyond him? He'd learned to give grudging respect to her discernment, and in this case it rang true with everything else that was going on in regard to Jesus. Could the gods . . . God . . . actually reveal Himself to people through dreams? Claudia had always been more spiritually attuned to the unseen realm. Could it be? Something inside him shifted. The note trembled in his hand. Implications far bigger than Jewish religious mandates and Rome's political muscle in this small parcel of the empire were clearly at work here.

The centurion caught his attention and motioned with his eyes back to the crowd. Pilate strode back to look down on the seething mass of people. For a couple of breaths, there was a silent standoff.

Then a priest whispered into the ear of one of the hired mob. Quickly the word spread and a shout went up, rolling into a roaring chant.

"Give us Barabbas. Crucify Jesus! Crucify Him! Crucify!"

Pilate was shocked. Surely they couldn't mean that! Returning inside, he spoke again to Jesus.

"Do you refuse to speak to me? Don't you realize that I have the power to either free you or crucify you?"

It was almost as if Pilate were saying, "Only say the word and I will release you." Once again Jesus could have escaped the cross, but He would not.

Jesus answered slowly and clearly. "You have no power over me that was not given to you from above. Therefore the ones who handed me over to you are guilty of a greater sin."

Pilate had his answer. Not even the might of the powerful Roman Empire could match the power of this one man who stood before him.

Pilate squared his shoulders, all the more determined to find a way to release the Nazarene.

But now the sea of writhing humanity before him took up the howling chant again.

"Crucify . . . crucify . . . crucify . . ."

Pilate stood there, waiting, unable to hide his contempt.

The Roman looked over to the priests at the front of the mob leading the calls for death. Seeing the hate in their eyes, hearing the savagery of their shouting, he found himself wondering about their religion, marveling that any religion would allow men to behave like this. "Do you want me to crucify your king?" he shouted.

"We have no king but Caesar!" shouted the chief priests. "Any man who sets himself up as a king is a rebel against Caesar."

The insinuation was clear: "Do you want word to get back to Rome that you have encouraged rebellion against Caesar?"

In claiming allegiance to Caesar, the Jews were guilty of their own charge of blasphemy.

The pressure mounted. Pilate had to decide. Whose side was he on? Rome's—the earthly kingdom? Or Christ's—the heavenly kingdom? Wealth, or fulfillment? Power, or peace? Emptiness, or answers? Saying yes to Jesus meant giving up all Pilate had worked for, all he had acquired. He could save Jesus' life or save his own.

Pilate gave in. He knew his answer in Jesus. He realized fully who Jesus was, but he could not pay the price of following Christ. The pressure of the shouts around him drowned out the pleading of his own heart.

Deliberately, scornfully, he called for a basin of water. Slowly he washed and then dried his hands. The action, unexpected, reduced the shouting of the crowd to a confused murmur. He spoke to them for the last time.

"I find nothing wrong with this man. Take him and do with him as you wish. The responsibility is yours."

The roar of approval made him shudder. He could at least tell his wife he had tried.

He handed Jesus over to be crucified.

His last act was a sign he ordered fastened to the cross: "Jesus of Nazareth, the King of the Jews."

Pilate had tried to wash his hands of his decision about Jesus, but he was never able to escape in his heart. Tradition tells us that Pilate ruled in Jerusalem for three more years, then was exiled where he later committed suicide. The frustration of his denial of Christ followed him to the end of his life.

We, too, are faced with the questions:

Whose side are you on?

What will *you* do with Christ?

The issues are the same for our hearts today as they were for Pilate's. We can try to save ourselves and wind up losing everything. Or we can say yes to Christ and find in Him everything our hearts long for . . . and immeasurably more.

What will you do with Christ?

The choice is yours.

BEYOND THE STORY
To Help You Think, Pray, Share and Do

1. Some people see religion as a crutch for the weak. How do you respond to that?

2. Pilate was turned off by religious people whose walk didn't match their talk. What have been some of your religious turnoffs? Why?

3. Have you ever had someone warn you because they had a dream or intuition about a situation? What did you do with their words?

4. Who do you know that appears outwardly disdainful of religion but might be secretly longing for the truth found in Christ? Take time to pray for them now. Keep praying, and keep living truth in front of them!

7

SUBSTITUTE ON SKULL HILL

(Barabbas)

MATTHEW 27:15-26

Rough hands jerked the prisoner to his feet. The chains that secured him to the wall of the dingy, stinking prison cell were unlocked, with only the leg and wrist irons still binding him.

"Come on, you scum, Pilate wants to see you," sneered the guard, hatred in his eyes. Only days before, one of the guard's best friends, a fellow Roman soldier, had died at the hands of the prisoner, killed by a thrust of his dagger. There was no man more hated among the Roman soldiers than Barabbas.

As he reached the entrance of the jail, Barabbas was prodded out the door into the sunlight. His hands instinctively covered his eyes at the intensity of direct sunlight for the first time since he had been thrown into a hole in the ground.

As his eyes adjusted to the light, Barabbas began the walk that he fully expected to be his last, surrounded by a wall of soldiers. He was a condemned man, and today he was going to die.

He had known it would come to this one day. For a while he had run free, leading a group of revolutionaries called the Sicarii, meaning dagger bearers, on a murderous revolt against the occupying Roman army. The more daring they became in sabotage and murder, the more his fame grew among the people of Palestine. To them, he was a patriotic hero, perhaps even a savior to lead the nation to freedom from the oppressive slavery of the Romans.

Barabbas smiled grimly to himself as he trudged along, jostled by the guards. Even his name, one that he had taken when he assumed leadership of the Sicarii, had helped to foster that illusion. "Jesus Barabbas"; "Jesus," meaning "savior," and "Bar-abbas," meaning "son of the father." He had believed it himself, feeling he was invincible. A savior who was son of the father, a messiah. Didn't his cause give him the right to do whatever it took to carry out his plan? When the objections of his conscience had tugged at his heart after another theft, another murder, another crime, his hatred and pride had squelched that inner voice until finally it grew silent. His own heart had become so callous that he could rationalize anything he did and make it seem the right thing to do.

Now all his rationalizations had been smashed by the reality of the chains on his wrists and ankles. In the cold light of justice, he was guilty, and he knew it. Still, the rage of a rebellious heart burned in him and smoldered in his eyes. Theft, murder, insurrection, treason, deceit—all those and other crimes were on the list of charges against him from the government of Rome; but he would die defiant. Never would he bow the knee to anyone! Barabbas answered only to himself.

The closely guarded prisoner arrived at the back of Pilate's palace, and the group waited until the governor came to meet them.

For a long moment, the eyes of the two men met—the cold, contemptuous gaze of the Roman, and the smoldering hostility of the prisoner. Barabbas stifled an urge to unleash a string of profanities at Pilate.

Finally Pilate spoke, his contempt undisguised. "Barabbas, you have been sentenced to die, and it would give me no greater pleasure than to run you through with my own sword right now. But according to custom, I release a prisoner at the time of your people's great religious feast. This year I am going to let the people choose. Jesus the Nazarene, whom many are calling the Christ and the Son of your God, has been accused of treason by your priests. They want Him crucified. I've been keeping track of Him for some time now, and the only thing He's guilty of is spreading a message of hope, forgiveness and love. I don't understand it, but this is clearly the work of jealous, hateful men, hiding behind the cloak of religion to kill an innocent man."

Pilate's voice had grown soft as he spoke about Jesus, but suddenly became hard as he addressed Barabbas. "You, however, are here because I could think of no one who deserves death any more than you do. If these people have any sense or decency at all, the choice of whom to free will be clear. You are flagrantly guilty of all you've been charged with, and much more. Come with me."

The news startled Barabbas. A chance at freedom was more than he could have hoped for. If enough of his supporters could be rounded up, they could swing the vote his way. A slender ray of hope broke into the blackness of his situation.

Climbing several flights of stairs, Barabbas found himself shoved onto a large porch looking out over the courtyard. To his right was Pilate's seat of judgment. On past him stood the other prisoner, Jesus of Nazareth, carpenter's son. Son of God.

Barabbas knew about the Nazarene. He, too, had been keeping track of his works and teaching. One of Barabbas's own men, Simon the Zealot, had defected to become one of Christ's disciples. Simon had come back to Barabbas a different man. Where anger and hatred had once dominated his personality, now there was a radical change. His eyes glowed with a new light as he eagerly told his former leader about the miracles he had seen. "There is a greater power than our hate, Barabbas," he said. "I have seen lives changed by the power of Jesus' love and forgiveness. We seek a new nation by revolution. Christ makes men new by regeneration. He starts with the heart, not with the sword. Come and follow Him, too, Barabbas. You can have the peace that I have found. Your way leads only to death. His way leads to life."

At the time, Barabbas had roughly dismissed his former follower. He was the leader! He would not submit to follow another! This weak-kneed way of love would soon fall by the wayside. Yet the reports of Christ's power and popularity continued to grow. Barabbas had watched with increasing interest. Perhaps there was something to all this. Perhaps what Simon had said was valid after all. Barabbas glanced over at Christ, seeing Him in person for the first time. It was obvious that He had been beaten. One eye was already swelling shut, His lips cracked and bleeding. His linen robe was soiled with dirt and spit. Yet He stood with head unbowed and a look of strength and peace on His features. If Barabbas hadn't known better, he would have thought that Christ was in control of the situation instead of Pilate.

Now they stood on the same judgment stand. One of them would die. Only one deserved to.

Pilate sat staring moodily at the mob throbbing with undertones of venom and hatred. He shuddered involuntarily with the thought of people whose religion could bring them to behave like this.

Suddenly he stood to his feet, and with his jaw thrust out, he spoke above the muttering of the crowd, pointing toward Jesus. "I have found this man, Christ, innocent of all wrongdoing. I will have Him flogged and released."

With that, the crowd howled in indignation. "NO! Crucify Him! Release Barabbas!"

Pilate tried again. "Would you have me crucify your king?" The chief priests moved forward and said with a veiled threat, "We have no king but Caesar. Crucify this one who pretends to be king!"

The crowd took up the chant, "Crucify . . . crucify . . . crucify!"

Pilate held up his hand, and the crowd grew silent. "All right, which one do you want me to release to you . . . Jesus Barabbas, or Jesus who is called Christ?"

Now the mob moved forward and pressed against the line of soldiers and screamed their desire to have Christ crucified and Barabbas go free. Their voices had reached a fever pitch, with almost a demonic overtone to their shouts. Pilate knew he could not control the mob. He gave them what they wanted. Barabbas would go free. Christ would become his substitute on Skull Hill. An innocent man would be nailed to the cross, and the guilty one would walk away.

When the freed criminal turned to look at Christ, their eyes met. Christ's look spoke volumes to Barabbas. *He knew who Barabbas was!* His heart was an open book to Christ, and there was invitation and forgiveness in those eyes.

The soldiers took off Barabbas's shackles, and with a bitter, "We'll get you another day," they went off to tend to the grim business of putting three men to death.

At first Barabbas stood stunned, massaging his wrists where they had been rubbed raw by the cuffs. Then he was surrounded by a group of his supporters slapping him gleefully on the back, telling him how glad they were that he was free. How glad that someone else would die in his place. After all, Barabbas was too valuable a man to die.

Barabbas wasn't feeling very valuable. He had seen the look on the face of Christ—His strength, His peace, His being of royalty in the face of that terrible throng, and suddenly Barabbas knew that Christ was no ordinary man. Barabbas had to find out more about Him . . . he had to! He who had said he would bow the knee to no man was being compelled to yield to *this* man, and Christ was about to die!

Tearing himself from the grasp of his admirers, Barabbas started after the procession that had gone to the courtyard. Lingering at the edge of the crowd, he watched in strange fascination as the Romans whipped and ripped Christ's back and legs to the bone. He watched, mouth open, as they slammed a crown of thorns on Christ's head and put the heavy cross on His shoulders. Then he was swept along with the mob down the narrow streets that led out of the city and to the hill called Golgotha, which means Place of the Skull. The jeering taunts stopped only for a moment as the hammer pounded the nails into the wood.

Barabbas continued to stare as Christ was suspended between earth and sky, between heaven and hell . . . on a cross marked for Him. He listened to Christ forgive those who had tortured Him, cowered with the rest of the crowd as the sky grew dark at noon. The sun refused to shine as its Creator was dying. He had seen many men die, but never had he seen one die like this. No threats of revenge. No screams of fear. No wild-eyed pleading of His innocence. He even made sure His mother would be cared for and spoke of Paradise to a repentant thief on the cross next to Him. Then, with a shout of victory, He put His spirit into His Father's hands. And then He was dead.

Tears ran unashamedly down Barabbas's cheeks. His pride, arrogance and hatred had flowed out of him with every drop of blood falling on the ground from the cross. He, Barabbas, deliverer of no one, deserved to die, not Christ! He was guilty, not Christ! Christ had been his substitute on Skull Hill, and Barabbas was free. There, in the dust of Calvary's slope, he dropped to his knees and vowed allegiance to the cause of his new Master and Leader. And he was free again, like Simon had said. He was free in his heart.

What Barabbas didn't know was that he was not the only person Christ substituted for on that cross, for Barabbas represents the whole of humanity. Guilty of treason against the holy King of heaven, we all have sinned and fallen short of the glory of God. We all deserve to receive sin's payoff: death and hell. We all have rationalized ourselves into feeling that our sins were for a good cause. We all have tried to be our own saviors, trying to overcome sin's tyranny in our own strength. We all have vowed to keep our right to be king of our own lives, yielding to no one. We all should have been nailed to the cross, paying the rightful due for our sins.

Yet, in Christ, the whole of the love and grace of God bore Barabbas's sins, and mine, and yours . . . and the sins of every man and woman that has ever lived. Christ alone could stand innocent before a Holy God and be declared blameless. Yet He chose to take Barabbas's place, and ours. He chose to be the substitute because there was no other way for people alienated from their heavenly Father to be able to come into right relationship with Him. That could happen only by the innocent dying for the guilty; only by the richness of His love paying off our debts as we stood bankrupt and destitute before God. Only because where sin abounded, grace did much more abound.

Today the opportunity that Barabbas had is still available to anyone.

The Savior who died in Barabbas's place on Skull Hill is our substitute too.

BEYOND THE STORY
To Help You Think, Pray, Share and Do

1. Barabbas was surprised by unexpected and undeserved mercy. Have you ever had that kind of experience in your life? How did it affect you?

2. Have you ever had someone take your place and accept the consequences you deserved? If so, how do you relate to Barabbas? If not, what does the story of Barabbas teach you?

3. Barabbas tried to bring change to his country through violence. How does that compare to what we see around us today?

4. How does the message of Jesus, of change through personal spiritual regeneration instead of political revolution, speak to us today?

WATCHERS AT
THE CROSS

1

A Hard Heart Under Religious Veneer

(Annas)

John 18:12-14,19-24

He hadn't trembled inside like this for over 30 years.

Outwardly, Annas appeared calm and in control. Inwardly, where only he and God could see, he was quivering in fear, reliving his worst nightmare.

It had happened 33 years ago. He'd been a young Sadducee then, with the ambition to become High Priest of the Sanhedrin driving his life. Things had been going according to the script he'd written for himself and followed without regard for obstacles or others.

Then *they* had shown up. They were eager, earnest and expectant. They'd come from a long distance, following a star that had suddenly appeared months ago—a star that signaled to them the birth of a great king being born in Judea. As he learned more about them, he found they were Magi from Persia, a land far to the east. They were much like him . . . and nothing like him. Like him, they were highly regarded in their own land. Like him, they wielded great religious and political influence. Like him, they were wealthy. Like him, they were respected in royal circles. Like him, they were considered guardians of sacred things.

But they were nothing like him. Although he wore all the outward trappings of organized religion, he knew nothing of a real relationship with the God of his religion. As a religious leader, he knew the sacred Scriptures by rote but had no desire for the written Word to be his resource and reality for life. Annas kept the "rules" of the Word as it best suited his ends. As a Sadducee, he could quote the necessary passages, but he denied any supernatural realities those passages might reveal. Yet here, standing before him, was a group of men who outwardly resembled him so much it was like looking into a mirror. But inwardly, he was nothing like them.

They confessed a hunger to know supernatural realities. One of them, named Caspar, spoke of his search for truth with such passion that it made Annas uncomfortable. They had searched for signs from nature and from the sacred writings of other religions, looking for clues to lead them to find and know the Creator. In fact, their search had led them to realize that there was the promise of knowing God as more than a distant Creator. Sacred Scripture, especially those of the Jews, declared that the Creator would actually come and live close to them and bridge the gap that sin had caused between Creator and creation. The Creator King would also become Redeemer and Savior.

When the Star had appeared, it was as if God was announcing to all who were paying attention that He was about to arrive. The Jewish writings called Him the Messiah or "Anointed, Sent One." They were so earnest in their search that they had covered a great distance at considerable expense, discomfort and danger in order to be among the first to see and worship this King. Caspar had said something that stuck in Annas's memory and bothered him long after they were gone. Caspar had said he knew about God in his head, but what he was longing for was to know God in his heart. For Annas, the distance between having religious knowledge in his head and a relationship with God in his heart was pronounced and protected. Head, yes. Heart, no. As a matter of fact, if the reality of Messiah was true, He represented a great threat to Annas's neatly ordered and tightly controlled religious world. The thought of God messing up his plans for power, position and wealth made him tremble inside.

Annas himself had been the one who had revealed the location of the Messiah's birth. He'd done it in the presence of the Magi, other religious leaders like him and King Herod. With looks of wonder, excitement and gratitude, the Magi had quickly left to traverse the last six miles of their journey to Bethlehem. Their search was nearly complete. The longings of their hearts would be met as they worshiped a newborn king. They had invited Annas and the other Jewish religious leaders to join them, and they were puzzled and confused when Annas and the others declined.

One look at Herod's face at the news told Annas all he needed to know. There was a hint of madness in Herod's eyes that told Annas the Baby would not live long in this world. If Annas wanted to stay alive, he'd steer clear of Bethlehem.

Not long after the visit of the Magi, the news that every baby under age two had been butchered alive in Bethlehem confirmed his hunch. The threat the Baby had represented to King Herod's reign and Annas's own ambitions had been exterminated. At least that's what Annas had thought and rested in at the time.

Only a few years later Annas realized his dream as he was appointed the High Priest of all Israel. It was the pinnacle of religious, political and material power in his nation. At one time, becoming High Priest was a position for life. When the hated Romans began their occupation, however, the High Priest now would serve at the appointment of the Roman governor. The Romans placed a high premium on a peaceful populace and a steady stream of tax revenues . . . and a cozy working relationship between Roman governor and Jewish High Priest was necessary for both sides to get what they wanted.

The Romans helped with civic infrastructure like roads and water systems. Herod, the "king" they allowed as a regional ruler, had also helped rebuild and expand the Jewish Temple. He had even built a special place in the Temple complex for the Sanhedrin to do their business. A renewed Temple had meant renewed spiritual pride, which was crucial to Jewish national identity.

The High Priest was allowed to conduct religious business under the umbrella of Roman jurisdiction in ways that affected the life of every man, woman and child in Israel. The High Priest would "keep the peace" for the Romans, and the Romans would allow the High Priest and the religious leaders to oversee the religious affairs of the people. Sanhedrin hands scratched Roman backs while Roman hands scratched Sanhedrin backs, and everybody was supposed to be happy. Politics and religion as partners was just good business . . . for Annas.

Annas was shrewd, smart, savvy and sly. His name meant "merciful" and "gracious," but no one ever accused him of living up to his name. He'd mastered the art of balancing and manipulating to his advantage the competing interests of various groups—the Roman outsiders and the different religious groups who formed an exclusive club of insiders—his own Sadducees, and the Pharisees and Scribes.

As High Priest, he was the head of the Sanhedrin, the highest ruling council of the nation, made up of 70 religious leaders, with the High Priest as head making the number 71. The Sanhedrin had legislative, executive, judicial, civil, criminal and ecclesiastical power over the nation. All of its judges, a blend of Sadducees, Pharisees and Scribes, had to be descendents of Moses to ensure racial, spiritual and political purity. They were the Supreme Court, the legislative body and the executive branch of government all resident in one ruling group.

They had a special meeting place called the Hall of Hewn Stone on the grounds of the Temple compound. They had strict rules of procedure that governed their actions as to what times they could meet, how they could conduct their business, how trials were prosecuted and how their decisions could be made. The Romans had taken away their ability to render a death sentence, but in every other way they continued their business as they had for decades, and business was good.

The law required many sacrifices to keep spiritual accounts current with God. Consequently, many people brought offerings and purchased animals for sacrifice. The Sanhedrin developed a special religious monetary system mandating the exchange of all other forms of money for "Temple" tender. Offerings at the Temple could only be made with that special currency developed by the Sanhedrin. Incoming religious pilgrims were required to acquire that special coinage at a high conversion ratio. All animal offerings, which by law had to be spotless, were first scrutinized by "Temple inspectors" who more often than not found the animal a worshiper had brought from home unacceptable, meaning they would have to purchase an "approved" sacrificial animal. Exchange rates for temple currency and approved animals were often 10 to 20 times the face value of "outside" money and animals. That exchange rate left pilgrims seeking forgiveness for their sins also empty in their pockets. But it brought huge financial gains into the Temple treasuries.

Annas and his family oversaw a religious and financial empire driven by greed and power. As a result, he and his family were hated by the common people who had no choice but to pay his price to worship at the Temple in order to make things right with the Lord. Helping people get right with God had made Annas incredibly rich. A religious system that had originally been founded on God's instructions and right intentions—all of which were to illustrate the redemption the Messiah would ultimately fulfill—had been corrupted by greed, hypocrisy and ambition. It was a form of godliness functioning as big business . . . done in God's name but without God.

It had not always been that way. There had been a time when the Sadducees saw themselves as the guardians of the written law and religious rituals. They oversaw the Scribes, whose jobs were to record accurately everything, from the sacred writings to the daily proceedings of the king. To maintain order, they felt they needed to maintain tradition. They received a great deal of training in the law and history of Moses and could recite sacred passages at great length. They did not, however, believe in the supernatural side of their religion. Resurrection from the dead and the existence of angels did not fit into their theological system.

With no spiritual side to their religion, they found themselves increasingly interested in and integrated with where they saw real power—in politics and the finances of the culture around them. Sadducees became the religious aristocracy—wealthy, politically connected and decidedly disconnected from meeting the needs of the common people they were supposed to serve. They used the worship needs of fellow Israelites to make themselves fabulously wealthy. With their accumulated wealth, they didn't need supernatural wonders. Their denial of supernatural beings such as angels and the reality of an eternal destiny did, however, put them at odds with the Pharisees, the other prominent religious group besides the Scribes.

The Pharisees were made up mostly of middle-class businessmen. Their distinction was their determination to be righteous through obeying religious laws and their dedication to oral traditions. Where the Sadducees honored the written law, the Pharisees had gone beyond the written law with commentaries and interpretations of the law. Their oral traditions were passed on from generation to generation, describing in minute detail how a person was to live out the law in every conceivable area of life. They saw righteousness as a result of self-effort, not trust in God. Their different social class and distinct view of theology often put Pharisees at odds with the Sadducees. Both still honored the Temple rituals, but the two groups spent extraordinary amounts of time pointing out their distinctives and arguing their differences. Both felt they were protecting tradition and pleasing the Almighty, but it was obvious even to the Romans that God could leave and their systems would never know the difference.

Although they would never admit it, that was just what happened. For 400 years, God had been silent. There were no supernatural signs or prophetic revelations. The Scriptures did promise that one day God would send them His Messiah to bring deliverance. The prophecies made good fodder for debate. Some argued the Messiah would be a powerful political deliverer to set them free from oppressive Roman rule. Others contended the Messiah would come to reign first in the hearts of people as a Savior from sin and then set up His rule on earth. The Sadducees and Pharisees debated, and the Scribes wrote it all down, but still they lived in spiritually impotent silence. There were still people who hungered to truly know God in the land, but Annas and the religious leaders were content to continue rituals, rake in the Temple profits and wrangle over the finer points of theology. People who wanted a real relationship with God were ignored. Besides, who needed God to provide for them when they had all the financial income and political influence they needed?

Who needed God to give them power to live a pure life when they had all the rules for external righteousness already spelled out for them?

Who needed God residing in their hearts when they could pride themselves in such a magnificent building "where God lived"?

Who needed God when adhering to religious regulations was more important than living out relationships fueled by holy love?

Who needed the wonder of knowing a God beyond comprehension when scholars had written down all that there was to know about Him?

Who needed God when you didn't believe in life after death, and resisting the Romans could mean certain physical expiration?

Annas had answered those questions for himself and decided he didn't need God ruling his life. It was astounding that the most important religious person in the land had determined that God wasn't important to him! Outwardly, no one could have guessed where Annas's true priorities lay. He wore his religious façade well, appearing to be a deeply spiritual leader. Inwardly, where only God and he could see, the reality was completely different. The purpose of life for him was power. Power was the ends, religion the means. Invoking God whenever Annas needed Him, in order to maintain his control, made embracing eternal things a matter of everyday expediency. Strict adherence to religious rules was expected for everyone else and yet conveniently adjusted to suit Annas's needs when situations warranted it.

He held his position as High Priest for nine years until a new Roman governor was observant enough to know how much power Annas really exercised. The Roman replaced Annas, but Annas outmaneuvered the governor by getting one of his own sons appointed to the position. Over the course of time, four of his sons and one son-in-law would hold the position, but Annas would still exert the power, maintaining control from his place as head of the leading religious family in the land. Thus, he managed power-sharing with the Romans through the surrogate leadership of his sons and son-in-law, Caiaphas, maintaining his status with political strategy and financial payoffs. The lines between cooperation, compromise and corruption were blurred to the point of being indiscernible; but without doubt, Annas was recognized as the one in control. Life was going just as he had planned.

For more than 30 years things had been going according to plan. His son-in-law, Caiaphas, had been High Priest for a dozen years, taking his cues from his father-in-law. Much older now, Annas didn't often leave his luxurious home. He didn't need to . . . people came to him there and all decisions came past him first. Caiaphas often walked across the courtyard that connected his residence with Annas's estate to confer with him before carrying out his duties. Caiaphas had the title but Annas still held the power.

Then reports began to come from Annas's network of informants spread out across the country. First from Capernaum, then from other places in the region of Galilee to the north—stories came to Annas's at-' tention of a Carpenter turned itinerant preacher who was perform- ing miracles along with His messages. At first Annas ignored them. Galilee was considered a poor backward area beneath the notice of prestigious Jerusalemites. Preachers making wild claims were not all that unusual. Often they were exposed as frauds in a short period of time, sometimes with a little help from operatives working for Annas who shaped public opinion according to Annas's wishes. Preachers came and went, but Annas remained in control.

Stories about the Carpenter from Nazareth, called Jesus, contin- ued to grow in size and scope. The messages influenced larger crowds, the miracles impacted increasing numbers of people. Local religious leaders where Jesus had ministered had first argued with Him but were often left shaking their heads in anger, frustration and unwilling won- der at what Jesus said and what He did. Eloquent words were one thing, passionate preaching another. But the supernatural power of Jesus was unlike anything they'd ever seen or heard about before.

People began questioning their local rabbis as to why people's lives were changed wherever Jesus went, and why nothing ever changed at their local synagogue. Even down into Jerusalem Jesus was the topic of conversation in homes, workplaces and wherever people gathered. Who was He? Extensive checks into Jesus' history found that He was from an average family who had lived in Nazareth for nearly 30 years. Jesus had apprenticed under his father, Joseph, as a master carpenter and then taken over the family business when Joseph died, taking care of His mother, brothers and sisters. Jesus, son of Joseph, was well re- garded in His community. He had led a very ordinary life until for some reason He had left home to begin a ministry that by all accounts had been nothing short of extraordinary.

Then some people began connecting the prophecies of Scripture about the Messiah with the person of Jesus; and when that happened, Annas really took notice. He made sure his spies were everywhere Jesus went with instructions to find something, anything, to discredit Jesus. Some initiated confrontations with Jesus designed to catch Him in a neatly laid verbal trap. Others instigated rumors to smear

His reputation. Nothing worked. To Annas's frustration, some of his spies actually became followers of Jesus! It was even said that two of the members of the Sanhedrin had become secret disciples of the Nazarene.

As the public popularity of Jesus expanded, the private pressure Annas felt enlarged as well. Caiaphas visited him more frequently, seeking his counsel about what to do with "the Nazarene problem." Until now the increasing fame of the Carpenter had not cut into financial profits, but when Jesus entered Jerusalem to adoring crowds shouting His praise and petitioning Him to save them at the beginning of Passover Week when Jerusalem swelled to a population of approximately 125,000 Jewish pilgrims from all over the world, Annas knew something had to be done. It seemed like the whole world was there to welcome Him . . . and worship Him!

Then Jesus arrived at the Temple and threw things into total disarray. Moving with magnificent anger and power, He'd turned over the tables of the money changers who were buying and selling in the midst of the sacred space, sending Temple currency ringing and rolling across the stone floor in all directions, moneychangers groveling and scurrying after the coins in consternation. Then He turned loose dozens of approved Temple animals from their cages in a flurry of feathers and fur, turning the entire religious market into chaos. Suddenly all eyes were upon Him, standing in the center of it all. His face alive with passion, His strong voice rang across the Temple. "It is written . . . My house shall be called a house of prayer, but you have made it a den of thieves." He'd quoted Isaiah and Jeremiah who had cried out against the religious corruption of their day; and those who had come to worship recognized what He was saying. Spontaneously, the common folks cheered! Pent-up frustration at being swindled in the name of religion spilled out. Finally someone had done something to stand up for them!

Priests and other Temple employees surrounded Jesus, shaking their fists in fury and shouting at Him in shrill voices. In the sharp exchange that followed, Jesus exposed their hypocrisy, used scriptural prophecy against them and declared them disqualified from Kingdom ministry. That was the last straw. This Carpenter had entered their controlled environment and challenged their authority in a very public and humiliating way! If this was allowed to continue, their whole empire was in jeopardy!

Annas summoned Caiaphas for an emergency strategy session. His decision was clear. Jesus had to go . . . not back to Galilee, but permanently. They then convened a quick meeting of the Sanhedrin in the courtyard between Annas's and Caiaphas's houses where Caiaphas declared that it was better for one man to die than for the whole nation to perish. It was, he pronounced in pious tones, their very way of life they were protecting. It was also protecting their pocketbooks, that issue unspoken but understood by all. Although they didn't take an official vote, the nodding of heads all around affirmed their assent.

Annas and Caiaphas retired to Annas's house with some of the key leaders and began to plot. The elimination of Jesus would have to be done slyly and skillfully. It could not be done in public. Jesus was much too popular with the common folk. Any move against Him where ordinary people could observe would cause a riot, which would get them in trouble with the Romans. No, it had to be done at some out-of-the-way place under the cover of darkness. But how would they know where to find Him? If only they had someone close to Jesus who could arrange such a scenario. Quietly the word went out through their channels that they would pay well for certain information, and then they waited.

A couple days passed. Jesus taught openly in the Temple to the delight of the huge Passover crowds, then retired across the Kidron Valley with His disciples to the home of friends. As evening shadows lengthened across his courtyard, Annas saw Caiaphas hurrying toward his house, nearly running in his haste, looking very undignified for a High Priest. It took his portly son-in-law nearly a minute to catch his breath when he arrived, but the news was well worth his effort. One of Jesus' inner circle of disciples, Judas by name, had offered to identify Him at a private location where He could be arrested in the dark. It was more than they had hoped for . . . and for only 30 pieces of silver—the price of a slave! Leaning forward to hear the news, the old man's eyes glowed with pleasure. Once again his plans were coming together according to his shrewd scheming. Quietly, Annas dictated his strategy to Caiaphas, then retired for the night. He'd need a good night's sleep this night, because he would get little sleep in the night to come.

The next day seemed to move far too slowly, although there was much going on because of Passover Week. Annas was preoccupied, irritable and distracted. Too many things could go wrong. He would not be at ease until this threat to his empire was eradicated.

Evening darkness finally arrived and an uneasy gloom seemed to settle on the city. Even in his spiritual dullness Annas could tell there was more going on than what natural senses could discern. He kept watch by his window, viewing his courtyard in the flickering light of the flaming torches that ringed it.

He and Caiaphas were leaving nothing to chance. Pilate had been alerted that in the morning they'd be bringing him a prisoner found guilty of a capital crime. A force of arrestors was milling about in the courtyard, a throng hundreds strong comprised of Temple guards, Roman soldiers and priests with small status but big aspirations. Finally, a small figure furtively approached Caiaphas, who nodded to the captain of the guards. The capture committee moved out, their torches blazing, lamps swinging, swords gleaming in the firelight, voices low and excited. Annas nodded to himself. The end had begun.

It was nearly two hours later when the captain of the guard finally requested an audience with Annas so that he could examine the prisoner. Annas had insisted on seeing Jesus first. It was his prerogative to be the first to look in triumph over the threat to his power.

He sat in the seat that was his throne and waited as they shoved the Prisoner in front of him. For a long moment they faced each other—a shriveled, hunched-over old man and a Nazarene standing tall, looking Annas squarely in the eyes. At first glance Annas wasn't impressed. The Carpenter was dressed simply. His clothes were smudged and soiled with spit and dirt. His hands were tied tightly behind Him. His face showed swollen evidence of sweat, strain and slapping. Jesus would have presented a pathetic sight if it hadn't been for the princely peace in His eyes. Annas was used to having people grovel and cower in his presence. There was no fear on Jesus' face. If anything, it appeared that Jesus was not impressed with Annas.

Annas leaned forward, glowering at Jesus. With his first question, the trial of Jesus began. Direct questioning of an accused person was not according to their rules, and no one could be declared guilty by their own words. Annas had bent rules before when he deemed it necessary; and before the night was done, he and the Sanhedrin would break many more.

"Who are you?" Annas's aged, gravelly voice sounded more like a croak.

Jesus looked steadily at him, saying nothing.

"What are your credentials to teach?"

"What are the names of your disciples?"

Annas's questions were met with silence.

"What is this doctrine you are teaching contrary to our law?"

No response.

"What right do you have to disrupt our Temple worship?"

Nothing.

"Do you realize who you are talking to?" He was beginning to get angry now.

Jesus continued to look steadily at him and then spoke patiently, as if reminding Annas of how the rules of the Sanhedrin were to be applied. "I've spoken openly in public. I've taught regularly in synagogues and in the Temple, where all the Jews come together. Everything that I've taught and done has been out in the open. I've said nothing in secret. Why are you questioning me in this way? You should be asking those who have heard me teach . . . they are the ones who know what I've said." Everyone in the room knew what Jesus meant—if you are going to question me, at least do it according to your own rules. A prisoner can't testify against himself. Others are supposed to do that.

Annas recoiled as if in shock. The keeper of the law was being instructed in the law! No one could remember anyone ever talking to him like this. One of the officers of the Temple guard stepped forward and slapped Jesus hard across the face, the stinging blow loud in the room. "How dare you speak to the High Priest like that?" he shouted angrily.

Jesus turned to look at the man, who involuntarily stepped back under His piercing gaze. "If I've said something wrong, prove it. But if what I said is right, then why are you striking me?"

With that, Jesus turned to look back at Annas, and waited.

In spite of himself, Annas looked away under the power of Jesus' presence. He frowned. This was not going as he expected. He'd had religious imposters claiming to be the Messiah come before him. Often they reacted like cornered animals, proclaiming their divine status with a torrent of angry words and hubris. Others had melted under pressure into a fearful puddle, begging for mercy from the High Priest. The Nazarene in front of him was unlike any person he'd ever met before. There was a calm certainty about Him, an unusual serenity in the midst of the immense stress He was under. In spite of himself, in another setting, Annas would have felt he was in the presence of dignity and royalty. Instead, his interrogation had been turned back on him. He had sought to gain the upper hand and look down on Jesus in triumph. Now he sat in his seat of power looking up at the Nazarene. Something was not right here.

His sharp old mind snapped back to attention. This was going nowhere. It was time for phase two of the trial. With a weary wave of his hand, he sent Jesus across the courtyard to where Caiaphas waited with as many of the Sanhedrin as they could gather in the middle of the night.

Wobbling down a private hallway with an aide at his side, Annas arrived at the back of the room where the religious leaders had gathered. From there he could observe the proceedings without too much notice. Caiaphas would be able to see him and respond to his cues. Caiaphas would be publicly in charge, but Annas would still be in control.

Once there, some of the elders protested the meeting of the Sanhedrin at night, a violation of their protocol. Criminal cases must be tried during the daytime and must be completed in the daytime. Criminal cases could not be transacted at any time during the Passover season. If a guilty verdict was reached, the punishment could not be pronounced until another night had elapsed, allowing time for feelings of mercy to surface. No decision was valid unless it was reached in legal session in their meeting place, the Hall of Hewn Stone. All evidence had to be validated by two witnesses who had been separately examined and had not had contact with each other. Perjury was punishable by death.

It was clear that they were not abiding by their own policies. Caiaphas held up his hands to quiet them, suavely saying that this was just an informal gathering to collect information that might lead to a charge against the prisoner. A real trial could take place at daytime. His reasoning sounded shallow. It was.

A procession of witnesses had been gathered, each exchanging their testimony for a price. Wild accusations and outright fabrications were delivered one after another. As each one spoke his piece he was questioned by Sanhedrin leaders. These were the sharpest legal minds in the nation, and even if the verdict was a foregone conclusion, they were still going to have some semblance of integrity in the proceedings.

Every testimony withered under cross-examination, every testifier slunk off into the shadows and out the door. With each failure, frustration mounted. Finally, two people said they had heard Jesus claim that He would destroy their beloved Temple and then rebuild it in three days. Under examination, even that accusation couldn't stand up. This was going nowhere. No one could be found to make any charges stick. No charge, no case. They were going to have to set Jesus free.

Caiaphas stood up menacingly, trying to intimidate Jesus. "Aren't you going to answer any of these charges? What do you have to say for yourself?"

Jesus stood secure and silent. Caiaphas grew red in the face, ready to explode from his frustration.

Caiaphas peered over the tops of the heads to the back of the room. Annas nodded to him, sending the signal to advance to the plan they had agreed upon. The "legal" way had not worked. They would have to resort to their final solution—completely illegal but absolutely essential. Jesus would have to condemn Himself.

Caiaphas drew himself to his full height, trying to make himself look taller. Pointing an accusing finger, he spoke slowly so all could hear, "I adjure you by the living God . . ."

Gasps rippled across the room. To be charged like this by the High Priest of God's people put someone under the most solemn of obligations. To not answer was considered an affront to God Himself.

"Tell us . . . are You the Messiah, the Son of the living God?" There it was, the real reason they wanted to kill Him. Religion versus God. Their religious machine against God's saving Messiah. Their way of life . . . or His. Little did they know it was the real reason He had come.

It was as if the entire room were holding its breath in anticipation. All Jesus had to do was deny the charge and He would go free.

They all knew that what Caiaphas had just done was illegal. No person on trial could either be asked or compelled to answer any question that would incriminate him. Still, what was at stake was so enormous that it superseded all their rules.

Jesus looked around the room, His eyes resting on each member of the Sanhedrin, then back at Caiaphas. Somehow, Annas felt that Jesus had lingered for an extra heartbeat or two when He looked at him, and again he felt uneasy.

"I AM!" Jesus' voice rang strong and clear with supernatural authority to every corner of the room. The shock of His words penetrated and reverberated in every heart. "I AM" was the name that God used when He identified Himself to Moses! "I AM" . . . the Eternal One . . . the One Who was, who is . . . who is yet to come . . . the One who causes all things to exist. The Son of God was standing in their midst!

Jesus continued, ". . . and you will see the Son of Man sitting at the right hand of the Almighty One and coming with the clouds of heaven." Another gasp. Now he had quoted Psalm 110 and the prophet Daniel! Both were considered prophecies about the Messiah, and Jesus had applied them to Himself! In that one sentence He had declared a stunning reversal to the inquisition. He was declaring to them that one day He would be sitting at the right hand of Almighty God in the place of power and He would be sitting in judgment over His accusers. They would be answering to Him! He had taken the highest titles for God's deity and given them to Himself.

Annas's suddenly felt faint. Caiaphas's eyes grew large and he took a deep breath to puff himself up. This was beyond what they could have hoped for! Not only had Jesus responded, but He had also made the clearest statement from their own Scriptures that He was God. It didn't matter whether the statement was true or not. This was not about truth, it was about accomplishing their predetermined plan to eliminate this threat.

Grasping the front of his richly ornamented priestly robe, a look of triumph in his eyes, he ripped the front downward, shouting in wounded indignation, "Blasphemy! He has claimed to be God! What need do we have for any further witnesses! You've heard the blasphemy from His own lips . . . what do you say to it?"

The rest of the Sanhedrin came out of their stunned shock with a roar. Standing to their feet almost as one, shouts of "Death . . . death to the blasphemer!" filled the air. Then they came at Jesus in a rush, surrounding Him, spitting on Him, smashing Him with their fists, shouting at Him. Their offended religious dignity demanded they uphold the law and the name of God. Their ferocity was supposed to be a mark of their spirituality, and they were "spiritual" with a vengeance.

Caiaphas allowed the ugly onslaught against Jesus to continue for a few moments, then called them to silence. He reminded them that legally they could not pronounce a verdict or a sentence until daylight, so he ordered Jesus be held in a stony hole behind his home until they could reconvene at daybreak in their official meeting place at the Hall of Hewn Stone. It would only be a couple more hours; then they could make it official.

Rather than go home, the members of the Sanhedrin stayed at Caiaphas's home, talking and eating. The gathered crowd in the courtyard was informed of the preliminary finding and the news began to spread across a sleeping city now suddenly awakened with startling news.

Annas remained seated, receiving the homage of the various Sadducees, Pharisees and Scribes as they declared their loyalty to him and to his office. Outwardly, he maintained his composure of being in command. Inwardly, he felt his foundation of control beginning to crumble. They had won, but his surge of triumph was short-lived. His finely honed intuition was warning him . . . what was happening where he couldn't see?

As the first hint of dawn became visible on the eastern horizon, Caiaphas had Jesus brought out of the below-ground cell where they'd been holding Him. He'd reconvened the Sanhedrin in their formal meeting place and placed Jesus once more before the seventy other members. Now that it was daylight they could make this "legal," even though they had broken almost every one of their own rules. Sitting in the three-tiered stone semicircle where every member could see each other, they voted one by one, from youngest to oldest as policy dictated. Annas would cast the last vote. He stood, hunched over by age but still commanding attention by his presence. His "Guilty" sealed Jesus' fate as far as the Sanhedrin were concerned. Now it was up to Pilate to carry out their death sentence. Annas had already paved the way for that to happen.

Leaving Caiaphas and other elders to deal with Pilate and see the process through to Jesus' death, Annas returned to his home. Messengers would keep him updated on the progress, but he would wait.

The morning was still young, but Annas felt old . . . so very old. He was weary and drained. This whole business had taken a great deal out of him. But by the end of the day they'd have Jesus eliminated, and life could get back to normal.

Reports came trickling back . . . Pilate tried to back out of their deal by sending Jesus to Herod, who then sent Him back to Pilate. Finally they applied pressure from several directions—inciting a mob to riot, insinuating Pilate's loyalty to Rome was in question, and at last Pilate gave in.

By nine in the morning a procession was headed for the place of public executions outside the city gate, a place known as "The Skull." Word came back that Jesus was now nailed to a cross. Annas fretted and waited.

At noon the sky went dark for no explainable reason, and Annas's uneasiness grew as he peered up into unearthly gloom.

At three in the afternoon, at the moment the Passover lamb was being sacrificed in the Temple, the earth shook beneath Annas's feet and a crack appeared across his marble floor. Minutes later a messenger arrived to confirm that Jesus was dead. Shortly after that came the sound of running feet, and then a red-faced priest appeared in the doorway. Ignoring proper protocol, gasping for breath, panic on his face, the priest stammered out an unbelievable report. The curtain that separated the Inner Court from the Holy of Holies—a curtain as thick as a man's fist—had been torn from top to bottom! The Holy of Holies, where only the High Priest could enter once a year, was now open! Other messengers came with astounding reports . . . rocks were split wide-open all over the region. Graves were thrown open and formerly dead corpses rose from their resting places alive!

With those reports, Annas trembled inside like he had more than 30 years before, after the visit of the Magi. Prophecies were coming to life before his eyes. His plans had succeeded, yet he felt outmaneuvered and somehow defeated. The last time, he had helped maneuver

Herod into killing babies with one baby in mind. He had failed. This time he had helped maneuver Pilate into making sure He was dead. Apparently, he had succeeded.

Annas sighed.

It had been a long Friday.

Hopefully now this Jesus as Messiah business was ended.

On Sunday he would find out it had only begun.

BEYOND THE STORY
To Help You Think, Pray, Share and Do

1. "Religion" can be big business. People are willing to spend lots of money for spiritual solace. How do you see that happening today?

2. Why did Annas, and religious leaders like him, feel threatened by Jesus?

3. If you had been in the crowd on the day Jesus threw out the mon-eychangers and confronted the corrupt religious practices going on in a house of worship, how would you have responded? Why?

4. If you know any people today that remind you of Annas, take time to pray for them. Ask the Lord to break down religious barriers so they can have a real relationship with Christ.

2

"KING OF MY HEART"
(The Centurion)

MATTHEW 27:43-54; MARK 15:6-39

On Sunday a great crowd had celebrated in exultation at the arrival in Jerusalem of the one they hoped would set them free . . .

Free from the tyranny of the hated Romans.

Free to rule their country again.

Free to do what they wanted to do.

The vast throng had formed a human entryway for Jesus of Nazareth as He rode in on a colt. They waved palm branches like festival banners and laid their coats on the roadway. It seemed that all of Jerusalem had turned out to cheer for Jesus of Nazareth. The city had never seen such a triumphal entry. It was a welcome celebration for a king.

By Friday, the city's complexion had completely changed. Cheers turned to jeers and insults. The shouts of "Hosanna" were now "Crucify Him!" It seemed that the whole city had changed their minds and hearts about Jesus. They had hailed Him as their Deliverer, their Christ; now they wanted to hand Him over for death as a criminal.

Much has been said about the masses of people who called Him Christ on Sunday and criminal on Friday. *It is amazing how fickle people can be when God doesn't measure up to their preconceived expectations.*

Yet the person who so greatly intrigues us as we view the crowd at the cross is the one person we know of who changed his mind the other way—who came to believe and definitively state that Jesus Christ is indeed the Son of God. In seeing who changed his mind, we are even more intrigued and amazed:

"And when the centurion, who stood there in front of Jesus, heard his cry and saw how he died, he said, 'Surely this man was the Son of God!' "

The centurion, the man who supervised the arrest, led the journey from the Sanhedrin to Pilate to Herod and back to Pilate, who oversaw the scourging that Jesus endured and then rode behind Christ to Calvary and made sure the crucifixion took place as ordered, *he* was the man who changed his mind and found Jesus as Son of God, and as Savior at Calvary. History tells us his name was Longinus. Later, legend tells us that after that day on Golgotha, he became a powerful witness for Christ and ultimately gave his own life for Christ in Cappadocia. How does a man make a decision like that? What does he have to tell us?

The meeting that Longinus had with Christ at Calvary was not his first. Actually, his knowledge of Jesus of Nazareth had begun some time ago. To him, Jesus was first a riddle. Longinus first began to hear about a carpenter who was attracting large crowds nearly three years earlier. As a centurion in an occupied land, it was his responsibility to keep tabs on potential threats to Roman rule. Any attempt at insurrection would quickly be brought to his attention and dealt with by the cold steel of Roman might.

Longinus had to deal often with many such threats in this little dusty and troublesome province called Palestine. The Jewish people had a fierce loyalty to their country and religion. They hated the Roman rulers with a passion, mostly in the name of their religion. Longinus wondered at a religion that could make people hate so. He remembered thinking that any religion he would ever have a part in would have love at its heart. He'd had enough hate to last any man a lifetime.

Thus, when a carpenter from a backward village called Nazareth began to create a stir, Longinus was curious. What would a common carpenter have that people could want? It puzzled him. Nonetheless, he began to gather information.

From the very first the reports about Jesus had been different than any others he had ever received. Apparently the carpenter had only a dozen close followers, and a few women who helped them from time to time. He didn't try to drum up crowds. Rather, He seemed to shy away from publicity. Yet, wherever he went, people gathered in large numbers. There were reports about his teaching—about God and the needs of the human heart—in a language all could understand. He didn't preach revolution or hate against the Romans; he spoke of regeneration of the heart by love.

Beyond his teaching, information kept coming about miracles taking place wherever Jesus went. Lame people walked. Blind people saw. Deaf people heard again. Crippled people were restored to radiant health. Demon-possessed people became sane and free again. He even heard that on two occasions, thousands of people had been fed when only a few loaves of bread and a couple of fish had been available. And then there were the stories about dead people coming to life—even a well-known man named Lazarus, who had been dead four days when he came back to life.

The more Longinus heard about this Jesus, the more concerned and confused he became. Who was this man, anyway? Longinus's superior, Pontius Pilate, was also growing uneasy. The carpenter was gaining a great deal of popularity with all kinds of people. Even tax collectors and prostitutes were coming gladly to follow Him. Wherever this Jesus went, people became different. He even was heard to forgive people their sins. Even a Roman centurion knew that only a god could do that.

When Caiaphas, the Jewish High Priest, and the other Jewish religious leaders came to strike a deal with Pilate to do away with Jesus, Longinus was surprised. Why would religious leaders want to orchestrate a murder? "It's either him or us," they said. "He had claimed to be equal with God—to be God's own Son. Our religion says that such a one must die. And beyond that, this man has taken our popularity with the people . . . and our religious business."

And so, after the carpenter's big entry to the city on Sunday, Longinus had been directed to arrest him in a garden just outside the city under cover of darkness. The carpenter offered no resistance—He even seemed to be expecting the rabble that came to arrest Him. Here they were, armed to the teeth, and Jesus received them with unarmed dignity and grace.

Jesus maintained that grace and dignity throughout a mockery of a trial before the Jewish ruling council and before Herod. It was before Pilate that things came different for Longinus. In that incredible interview, he watched Pilate talk to Jesus, now bruised by repeated blows, His garment soiled and dirty from rough handling and spit. Yet it was Jesus who stood with a regal calm, who seemed in control of the conversation. He said he was a king . . . not of this world, but a king for all who sought truth. Pilate seemed to be actually afraid of the quiet strength of the Carpenter.

So He thought He was a king, did He? Longinus hadn't minded Jesus being a teacher, or even a miracle worker, but this business of being a king—well, Jesus would not be *his* king. Caesar got his share of Longinus's time, but after that, his life was his own. The troublesome carpenter had ceased to be a riddle; He had now become a rival. Longinus had the uneasy feeling that Jesus would be king of all his life, not just parts of it. He could not, no, he would not relinquish his rights to himself to this Jesus.

And so Longinus agreed with the desire of the people to crucify Jesus. Perhaps this carpenter would show His true colors under the pressure of crucifixion. Then Longinus could dismiss Him as just another deluded religious fanatic and get back to normal life. He watched Jesus walk on unsteady feet the distance to Skull Hill with no malice in His eyes. No hatred or fear on His lips. Longinus, his soldiers and the condemned men climbed to the top of Golgotha with the stench of putrid smoke wafting up from the garbage dump on one side and on the other side the barrage of shouting from a massive crowd overcome by the frenzied, demonic anticipation of the suffering they were about to see. He watched Jesus wince in agony when they threw Him down on the cross, the bloody, shredded skin of His back ripped even more by the rough wood. Then, as the ringing of hammer on spike filled the air, even the most hardened in the crowd were shocked into stunned silence.

It is a gruesome thing to hear nails being driven through human flesh.

As the nails pierced Jesus' flesh, Longinus waited for the pain to burst the Galilean's calm. He waited for the cursing, the threats, the pleas for mercy and the blasphemy that he was accustomed to. He had seen a lot of men die, and death always revealed a man's true character. With all the taunts and mockery coming from the frenzied crowd, Jesus would crack even sooner.

But He did not. In spite of the incredible pain, Jesus still had that unearthly dignity and strength. Longinus moved closer and watched. There was something happening here that he had never seen before.

Jesus looked at the crowd and at him and prayed, "Father, forgive them, for they know not what they do." What was this? A man praying for the forgiveness of the very people who had treated Him so terribly and unjustly?! That was not human nature. Suddenly it struck Longinus right between the eyes, shaking him to the depth of his hardened heart. It was *not* human . . . it was divine. This man might really be who He said He was. Only God in a man could be handling all this like Jesus was. A hunger began to grow in the Roman's soul to talk to Jesus—not just to gather information but to talk about the needs of his heart. But it was too late. Jesus was dying before his very eyes, and dying like a king sacrificing Himself for the freedom of His people.

Time oozed out like the blood dripping off the rugged wood of the cross. Two hours passed. Then three. Suddenly a heavy darkness fell over the land, as if nature itself could not bear to watch what was happening. Longinus shuddered. Was this man Lord over nature too?

Jesus forgave one of the thieves on the cross next to Him. He confidently assured the man, "This very day you shall be with me in Paradise." He took care of the needs of His mother. What love to care so much in the midst of such pain! This was strong love, sacrificial love, pure love. Longinus had never seen love like this before.

At the six-hour mark, Jesus threw back His head and shouted in a strong, triumphant voice. It was not the whimper of a helpless, defeated, dying man. It was the shout of a victorious warrior who had just conquered his enemies.

"TETELESTAI! IT IS FINISHED! Father, Into Your hands I commit my spirit." And with that, Jesus lowered His head and died. The ground shook, and something in Longinus's heart was shattered. All his stubborn, cynical pride was broken by a Man who was much stronger than he could ever be. He was humbled by love so strong and selfless. He was stripped to his sinful core by such holiness in the midst of such corruption.

There in the midst of the crowd, Longinus took off his helmet. He yielded allegiance to his King. As he looked up at the limp figure on the cross, his eyes filled with tears and in a voice full of awe, he said, "Surely this man was the Son of God!"

Christ had been a riddle. Then He had been Longinus's rival for the kingship of his heart. But now . . . now it all fit together. This man was the Son of God, and He had become his Redeemer. The crowd had crucified Him. Longinus now crowned Him King of his life.

Down through time, untold numbers have stood at the foot of the cross just as Longinus did. At the cross, all our rationalizations, rebellion and reservations are removed by the power of Christ's incredible sacrificial gift of love. Millions have looked up at the cross with awe and humility and said, "Surely this man *is* the Son of God . . . my Savior . . . my King."

Look up at the cross. See the One who hung there for you. You've heard Longinus's words.

Now, what do you say?

BEYOND THE STORY
To Help You Think, Pray, Share and Do

1. The Centurion was caught between his duty and his growing understanding of who Jesus really was. Have you known times when you felt like you've had to choose between duty and God? How did you handle those situations?

2. Many people "hear" about Christ over a period of time before actually meeting Him up close. What is your story about getting to know Christ? How might you relate to the Centurion?

3. Watching how Jesus died was the final proof for Longinus that Jesus truly was the Son of God. Oftentimes, watching Christians suffer is a powerful witness of the reality of Jesus' true identity. What experience have you had watching the witness of someone who is suffering in the name of Christ? What opportunities have you had to display God's grace to others in your suffering?

4. The ground is level at the foot of the cross. No matter who we are or what our position, we are all equally in need of God's grace and salvation. Have you stood at the foot of the cross and declared Jesus as your Lord?

3

BORN AGAIN AT THE FOOT OF THE CROSS

(Nicodemus)

ISAIAH 53; JOHN 3:1-7

He stood squinting into the late morning sun, the look on his face a mixture of horror and awe.

Hanging above him, suspended between earth and heaven, three men were nailed to crosses of rough, blood-soaked wood. Although there were three men, the gaze of Nicodemus was singularly drawn as if by a magnet to the man on the middle cross. He could not take his eyes off of Him. As he stared in wonder and terror at the horrifying spectacle in front of him, it seemed as if an unseen curtain was drawn aside so that he could see far beyond the physical agony he was witnessing.

There was far more going on here than met the natural eye.

Words hidden in his heart for many years began to rise to the surface of his memory. It was as if he could hear the voice of a prophet speaking across seven centuries, revealing to him the full impact of what was taking place in front of him.

More than two years had passed since Nicodemus first heard about Jesus, the carpenter from Nazareth. As a member of the ruling religious party, word came to him from various sources that kept him informed of the religious news of the day.

At first there were reports about a powerful meeting of Jesus with a rough, fiery prophet the people had named John the Baptist. The sky had opened up with light. Some said they actually heard a heavenly Voice when John baptized Jesus. Not long after, stories came in rapid succession of people being healed and fed and delivered from demons. There were stories of how Jesus could out-teach and out-preach any trained scholar or rabbi. It seemed that He was more than willing to travel outside traditions so carefully crafted by men. Yet, He always lined up with the Word of God. The more Nicodemus heard, the more he felt drawn by a desire, no, a *need* to talk to this man and try to understand Him.

He stood at the edge of the crowds that came to listen to Jesus teach, overwhelmed both by the number of people who came to hear Him, and by the content of Jesus' messages. Though he would admit it to no one else, Nicodemus saw in Jesus something he did not have but had hungered after—a freedom to love people, a power to change lives and most of all a relationship with God that could only be described as intimate and real.

He met Jesus face to face for the first time under the cover of darkness in order to protect his reputation. Jesus did not seem impressed by his title or position, but instead welcomed Nicodemus much like a kind doctor welcomes a patient coming for a health examination.

In asking his question, "How do you do the things you're doing . . . you must be a teacher from God . . ." Nicodemus's voice poorly masked his longing.

With a slow, wry smile, Jesus had responded to Nicodemus, His answer at first startling, then puzzling. Jesus simply said that what Nicodemus really needed was to be born again. In fact, He said, it was the only way that Nicodemus or anyone else could enter into and experience the kingdom of God.

Nicodemus could not resist the urge to ask the meaning of such a statement. How could a man be born again? He couldn't enter a second time into his mother's womb . . . What Jesus was asking was impossible!

Again that slow smile from Jesus. It was, He said, a spiritual birth that was needed for a person to enter the family of God. It could not happen by human effort or religious ritual. It could only happen in simple faith. And then, reminding Nicodemus of an example from the Holy Word, He said, "Just as Moses lifted up the snake in the desert, so the Son of Man must be lifted up, that everyone who believes in Him may have eternal life." His words puzzled Nicodemus but the pull on his heart toward the truth Jesus spoke increased.

"The Son of Man must be lifted up . . ." Suddenly those words came back to Nicodemus's memory so clearly that he thought he was hearing them said again, and all the pieces of prophecy regarding God's Messiah, the Lamb of God, fell into place before his eyes.

He looked around, wide-eyed, to see if anyone else was reaching the same conclusion he was. Across the seething mob of people he could only see a handful of people weeping, undoubtedly a few of Jesus' family and followers. The rest of the huge crowd, better described as a mob, hurled cruel words, stinging accusations and venomous insults at Jesus. He saw faces contorted with anger and rage, eyes black with wicked delight at the spectacle before them, laughter demonic in its enjoyment of the unspeakable suffering Jesus was enduring. Nicodemus shuddered and shook his head.

Didn't they understand what was taking place? Didn't they comprehend the enormity and significance of what was happening? The greatest single event in human history . . . and they saw . . . nothing! Their eyes and their hearts were blinded by prejudice and pride and self-protection.

Then the words of Isaiah the prophet forced themselves to the front of his consciousness again, and Nicodemus saw the whole incredible, horrible drama come alive.

"But, oh, how few believe it! Who will listen? To whom will God reveal His saving power?

"See, my servant will act wisely; he will be raised and lifted up and highly exalted. Just as there were many who were appalled at him—his appearance was so disfigured beyond that of any man and His form marred beyond human likeness . . . "

The night before, Nicodemus had seen that calm, regal, powerful face as Jesus had responded to the brusque question of the Chief Priest at the trial. "Are you the Messiah, the Son of the Blessed One?"

All Jesus had to do was deny it and He could have gone free. Instead He had looked around the room at the gathered men and then straight at the Chief Priest. His answer rang out across the room.

"I AM!"

Nicodemus watched helplessly as the men of the Sanhedrin, religious leaders, refined and dignified, went up to Jesus and began to spit on Him, covering His face and robe with phlegm. Then they had begun to strike Him again and again, fists clenched in malice. Jesus' lips began to swell, His nose began to bleed, His eyes began to blacken, His face became disfigured as those men tried to pound their judgment into Jesus for having the audacity to claim to be God.

Nicodemus was embarrassed and repulsed by such behavior exhibited in the name of religion.

"He was despised and rejected by men, a man of sorrows, and familiar with suffering. Like one from whom men hide their faces He was despised, and we did not appreciate His worth."

Nicodemus followed the growing mob as they dragged Jesus to see Pilate and howled for His death. He turned his head away as they led Jesus to a courtyard, stripped Him naked and then tied Him, bent over, to a post.

He knew what was coming.

The scourging began. Some who were going to be crucified never made it past the whipping. They were considered the fortunate ones.

After the appalling spectacle in the courtyard, Nicodemus was carried along by the surging tide of people cramming the narrow streets of the city as they led Jesus past the city gate to a hill called the Skull, to be crucified. He watched Jesus try to carry the rough, splintered cross on His shredded back, saw Him fall, saw someone else carry the cross up the hill.

With horror he witnessed the crowd offer to help nail Jesus to the cross, roaring with a fiendish relish at what was yet to take place.

He watched as the soldiers threw Jesus to the ground, mixing dirt with the shredded flesh of His back, and then laid Him on the rough, splintered crosspiece and spread His arms across it with His palms facing up.

The crowd's jeering grew louder as they watched a soldier bring forward a bucket of rusty spikes, well used from many other crucifixions. The shouting stopped as the sharp metal sound of hammer on spike rang through the air. The crowd was shocked and stunned to hear nails being driven through human flesh. Even the hardest of them grew silent.

As the soldiers lifted Jesus heavenward and dropped the cross into a hole, with a dull thud, the roaring began again. After all that Jesus had been through, it was hard to recognize Him as a human being.

But the worst was yet to come. It was not a sight for the faint of heart or the queasy of stomach.

Of all the ways man has devised to bring death to another man, crucifixion is among the slowest, most agonizing, most excruciating and despicable. The scourging was intended to hasten death, yet some men lasted up to a week hanging from a cross.

The body of the victim was suspended to the wooden cross by spikes driven through the bones of the wrist and then through the feet, with the knees slightly bent. All the weight of the prisoner hung on those spikes, and the position of the body would not allow the person to inhale. In order to do that, the victim would have to push himself up, throwing all his weight on the nails driven into the feet, rubbing his back against the splinters of the wood until he could catch a breath. Then, when the pain on the feet became too great, he would sag down, putting all the weight again on the wrists, sending screaming spasms of pain through his body. Again and again this cycle of pain and agony was repeated until the victim was too weak to continue. Death was often the result of a loss of blood and asphyxiation.

Yet Jesus bore it all without anger or cursing or threats . . .

"He was oppressed and afflicted, yet He did not open His mouth; He was led like a lamb to the slaughter . . ."

The sun beat down on them, time moving minute by minute, like the drops of blood from Jesus' wounds, making darker smudges on the ground beneath the cross. Nicodemus saw Jesus' lips move, and he strained forward to hear His words. Jesus' voice was clear, yet strained with pain, as He looked out across the sea of depraved humanity drinking in with delight the suffering He was enduring.

"Father, forgive them, for they do not know what they are doing."

Forgiveness? The words struck Nicodemus. In the face of such monstrous injustice? Incredible. Impossible! Yet, there it was, undeniably and deliberately given by Jesus to those who deserved it least.

At that same moment the sun grew dark. An eerie, inky blackness covered the land. It seemed as if creation itself could not bear to watch its Maker being put to death by the very ones He came to redeem and restore. Again, Isaiah whispered to Nicodemus across time.

"We all, like sheep, have gone astray, each of us has turned to his own way; and the LORD has laid on him the iniquity of us all . . ."

Nicodemus found himself repeating the words from memory. He looked again, more closely, as if trying to read Jesus' mind. The evidence of physical suffering was horribly apparent, yet it seemed that Jesus was bearing a much greater weight than just that of His own body. It seemed that the weight of humanity was upon Him—the abuse, the wounds, the lies, the pain, the pride, the prejudice, the greed, the lust—all our iniquity was being laid on this sinless Man!

"Yet it was the Lord's will to crush him and cause him to suffer . . . [making] his life a guilt offering . . ."

Then Jesus suddenly looked up, His face full of fear. He looked upward as if trying to find someone, and His voice cried out in desperate anguish, "My God, my God, why have you forsaken me?"

Jesus had been able to bear all the other anguish, but His greatest agony came in being cut off from His Father. At the crucial point in the most important event in human history, God Almighty, the Holy One, had to turn away for the first and only time in all eternity from the One who had been made sin on sinful humanity's behalf.

"But he was pierced for our transgressions, he was crushed for our iniquities; the punishment that brought us peace was upon him, and by his wounds we are healed."

With a look of horror, frustration, wonder and awe, Nicodemus pushed his way as close as he could to the cross. The full impact of the agony of Jesus' suffering crashed in on his own heart.

The agony of the physical suffering.

The agony of the rejection of those He came to save.

The agony of the weight of the totality of humanity's sins being brutally pushed down on Jesus.

The agony of the separation between Father and Son in order to do what had to be done to save us.

The agony of Nicodemus's own sinfulness and guilt.

There was only one response in the face of such incredible agony mixed with such infinite grace . . .

Nicodemus dropped to his knees, and suddenly he experienced the reality of what Jesus had said to him that first night . . .

When a man is born again, he sees the kingdom of God.

BEYOND THE STORY
To Help You Think, Pray, Share and Do

1. There are many prophecies in the Old Testament that point to Jesus as the true Messiah. How many are you familiar with? Make it a point to get to know prophecies found in passages such as Isaiah 9:1-6; Isaiah 53; Psalm 22; Genesis 3:15; Zechariah 9:9; Micah 5:2-5. Only Jesus Christ could have fulfilled all those prophecies! Get to know them. This will help you base your faith on solid evidence both from Scripture and history.

2. For many people, the thought of Christ being crucified is more a sanitized movie version than the ugly reality of what really happened. As you read about the true horror of crucifixion, what thoughts and responses came to your heart and mind?

3. Have you experienced the new birth Jesus described to Nicodemus? If not, why not now? With a humble, honest heart, you can pray a prayer something like this and be born again . . .

> *Lord Jesus, I need You. I've been going my own way, but now I want to follow You. I believe You love me and gave Your life for me. I'm truly sorry for my sins and ask You to forgive me. Please come into my life . . . from this moment on I choose to follow You. Thank You for forgiving me, for making me a member of Your family and for a home with You in heaven someday. Amen.*

4. If you prayed that prayer, welcome to the family of God! Make sure you tell someone who will want to celebrate that decision with you! Who are you going to tell?

4

Darkness Becomes Light
(Mary Magdalene)

LUKE 7:36-50

She stood at the foot of the cross, the overflow of a broken heart streaming down her cheeks. The events of the past evening and morning had been a nightmare as her world had come crashing down around her. Behind her, the crowd shouted at and taunted the man on the middle cross, their faces contorted with a demonic glee, their words vile and putrid. The mass of people was a swirling sea of hatred, but she had eyes only for her Master, suspended by long nails to the rough wood. She was close enough to see the blood run off the deep wounds and drip onto the dusty ground, to see the spasms of pain rack His body as He struggled to breath. Death by crucifixion was a slow, torturous asphyxiation, the most barbaric means of execution man had ever devised, and Jesus the Christ was suffering the full weight of humanity's sin as well.

Suddenly the sky grew dark, as if the sun itself refused to give its light in the face of such a travesty. The crowd grew quiet, frightened by the midnight darkness at high noon. Even the soldiers turned to look at the man on the middle cross, stopping their gambling and horseplay. They had crucified hundreds of men, but never before had such an event occurred. There was something supernatural happening, and the centurion looked uneasily into the eyes of Christ, as if searching to understand something beyond his experience.

Jesus moved His head back on the cross, as a man sick with fever moves against a hot pillow. Then His lips moved, His voice weary but without malice. "Father, forgive them, for they know not what they are doing."

Forgive. For Mary Magdalene, that word triggered a flood of memories . . .

She remembered the first time she had heard of Jesus of Nazareth. It had been over two years ago, when the gossip began to circulate around her town about the Man from Galilee. They said He spoke with a sense of authority and wisdom that had not been heard in people's memories. Even beyond that, wherever He went, miracles seemed to take place. The blind saw. The diseased were healed. The crippled were made whole.

It had not impressed her. She had heard about men with big reputations before, but the man in person never lived up to the reputation. The fact that He was religious didn't matter much either. Some of the so-called religious leaders had been customers of hers, purchasing a few moments of pleasure before donning their robes and heading back to their positions of influence and security. Yes, she had many customers, a number of acquaintances that were part of that lifestyle, but no one to really call friend, no one that she could really trust because they genuinely loved her. In spite of her outward appearance of well-being and happiness, inwardly she was desperately lonely. The "good" people scorned her wherever she went in public, telling their children to stay away from people like her. No one had ever invited her to come to their house or visit the synagogue to worship with them. Apparently they considered her beyond salvaging. Even God didn't want to have anything to do with her.

One day she had gotten up and looked at her reflection in the pool of water in her basin. She wasn't very old, but the lifestyle of sin had aged her beyond her years. Her face, growing weathered and wrinkled by a hard life, mirrored her heart. Even extra makeup would not preserve her fading beauty for long. Then, even her customers would not desire her, and life would be over. She had looked at her face in the water's reflection that morning and wept. She felt degraded, her inner life dirty with decisions she could never take back, her soul dark and empty. There had to be more to life than this! But where? How? Who?

In her emptiness she had turned to the spirit medium who lived on the wrong side of town like she did. The old woman had greedily taken her money and then given her some words to chant to a god who would keep her young and bring her good fortune. There was darkness about the whole situation, but as she followed instructions, she felt a power that she had not sensed before. As the days went by, she opened herself up to the dark forces more and more, until one day she realized that she was not controlling those forces, they were controlling her. It was then that her last shred of hope was gone. She was lost . . .

> disillusioned,
>> degraded,
>>> desperate,
>>>> demon bound,
>>>>> dull despair was her daily reality.

The talk about the carpenter turned preacher continued to grow, and she began to really take notice when she heard what kind of people He was willing to associate with. They said He was as much at ease with tax collectors and prostitutes as He was with rich men and powerful leaders. He treated everyone the same way, never condoning sin but not being condescending either. He preached that people were to turn away from their sins and believe in Him. Some had even said that He had told people that their sins were forgiven, and their lives had been completely changed. Some even called Him the Messiah, the Son of God. He claimed to forgive sins? Even Mary knew that only God could do that . . .

Suddenly a spark of hope began to dawn deep in the recesses of Mary's heart. Perhaps He was different from all the rest. Perhaps He could set her free from her past and cleanse her from the deep, dark stains of sin. Perhaps there was a future for her. Perhaps God could salvage something from her life after all.

And then, one day, Jesus came to her town! The city was buzzing with the news. Mary ventured out of her house to try to see Him, but crowds constantly surrounded Him. If she could just talk to Him, she would ask Him if she, too, could find this freedom He had offered to those who would follow Him. If she could get close enough even to see Him where there would not be a crowd of people, maybe then . . .

She heard Simon, a prominent local Pharisee, invite Jesus to eat supper at his home that evening. Just a few friends, he said, so they would have a chance to hear more of what Jesus was teaching. The Master graciously accepted.

When she returned home, a plan began to form in Mary's mind. The years of frustration and desperation moved her to a crisis point of decision. She *would* see Jesus! She didn't care what anyone else thought or said, she must see Him, talk to Him, ask Him . . . "Please forgive me too." But what could she give Him? She must have something to pay Him for His services. She had seen enough of life to know that nothing came free. She had a jar of fine alabaster with some expensive perfume. Perhaps that would do.

The night air was dark and cool as she walked the streets to Simon's house. The dark forces seemed to try to turn her back, resisting her every step. Yet hope drew her on, and another Power helped her against the tide of darkness.

Finally, she reached the door of Simon's house. Taking a deep breath, she stepped inside. As her eyes adjusted to the lamplight, she saw a number of people reclining at a table, eating a meal. As they became aware of her presence, conversation stopped, faces registering surprise, shock and disgust. All except one face.

When Mary's eyes met those of Jesus, she had never had a man look at her that way before. She was used to the look that appraised her body. But Jesus instead looked right into her heart. He knew her! She sensed that every bit of her life was an open book. He knew her! And yet He did not reject her. There was an unspoken openness, yes, even acceptance in the eyes of Jesus. In spite of who she was, in spite of what she'd done, in spite of everything, she sensed that she was at last loved genuinely, unconditionally.

The floodgates of her heart burst open as she ran to the table and fell at the feet of Jesus, weeping brokenly. "Please forgive me, please forgive me," she begged softly through her tears. "If You are all they say You are, please take this gift as my payment to You." Her tears and the expensive perfume mingled on the feet of Jesus, making small tracks through the dust. She began to wipe His feet clean with her hair.

The room had grown silent, a sense of electricity in the air at this incredible turn of events. No woman like this had ever been in Simon's house before! Didn't Jesus know what kind of person she was? She was a sinner! She was not fit to be in the company of good people. Simon said as much under his breath, thinking no one could hear. The others murmured in their beards, apparently in agreement with the sentiment of Simon.

For a long moment the only sound in the room was the soft sobs of Mary. Then Jesus turned and looked deeply into the eyes of Simon and spoke. "Simon," His voice was not unkind but carried a sense of disappointment, "I have something to tell you."

"Tell me, Teacher," Simon said.

"Two men owed money to a certain moneylender. One owed him a year and half's wages, and the other less than two months. Neither of them had the money to pay him back, so he canceled the debts of both. Now which of them will love him more?"

Simon shifted uneasily in his seat, avoiding Jesus' eyes, beginning to get the emphasis of Jesus' story. "I suppose the one who had the bigger debt canceled."

Jesus nodded. "You have judged correctly."

Then Jesus motioned toward Mary and said to Simon, "Do you see this woman? I came into your house. You did not give me any water for my feet, but she wet my feet with her tears and wiped them with her hair. You did not give me a kiss, but this woman, from the time I entered, has not stopped kissing my feet. You did not put oil on my head, but she has poured perfume on my feet. Therefore, I tell you, her many sins have been forgiven, for she loved much . . . for he who has been forgiven little loves little."

Simon's face grew hard, and he drew his robes closer around him.

Then Jesus turned to Mary, and lifting her face in His hands until His eyes met hers, said slowly and distinctly, "Your sins are forgiven. Your faith has saved you; go in peace."

For a moment, Mary didn't understand. He hadn't asked anything from her. He had not given her a list of things to do in order to earn her forgiveness. He had simply and freely forgiven her completely. She didn't deserve it and hadn't earned it, and yet He had in one powerful act of love wiped clean her past and given her what she had never experienced before . . .

 a clean conscience,
  a sense of worth,
   a sense of being accepted by God,
    of belonging
     of being really, truly loved.

Then her heart caught hold of what had happened. Suddenly she was *free*! Free from the dark forces. Free from the loneliness. Free from her sinful lifestyle. Free to follow her new Master and Savior. Mary turned to go, a changed woman, delivered from an old life to one so fresh and new that she felt as if she had been born all over again. The next day she joined the rest of those following Jesus and became one of His most devoted disciples.

The sound of Christ's voice brought her back to the present moment at Calvary. As He looked up, His voice sounded triumphant. "It is finished! Father, into Your hands I commit My spirit." And with that, He lowered His head and gave up His spirit.

Deep inside, Mary sensed something she had not understood fully until that moment. She should have been on that cross. She had deserved to die, not Him! Yet He had gone in her place, paying a penalty she owed for sin. That was how much her forgiveness had really cost. That was how valuable she was to Him. That was how much she was loved.

The story of Mary Magdalene doesn't end at the cross. We meet her again on Easter Sunday, the first to meet the risen Christ. But her story is really all of our stories, in a very real sense. We are all sinners, whether our sin is as outwardly visible as Mary's; we are all lost and without hope as long as we are without God. Yet we all, like Mary, can receive from Christ such a love that is

unconditional,

unearned,

undeserved,

that He is willing to forgive us completely. That forgiving love doesn't come cheap. It cost Jesus Christ His very life to make it possible for us to become acceptable to a holy God and become part of His family. It is free to us, but it cost God everything.

We, like Simon the Pharisee, can frustrate that incredible, wonderful love by looking at our own goodness and refusing to yield our lives to Christ. God's offer is open, available, free to all who will come in sincere, honest repentance and faith.

What do you call love so amazing, so divine? What do you call forgiveness so complete? There's only one word that can really describe it for us: grace.

Mary Magdalene discovered that when sin overwhelmed her—when she came to Jesus—His grace overcame it all.

When we come to Jesus like she did, in humility and honesty, we'll find His grace can do the same for us.

BEYOND THE STORY
To Help You Think, Pray, Share and Do

1. Some people feel they've done such bad things that they can't be forgiven. Have you ever felt like that? What do you think Jesus wants to say to you?

2. "Those who have been forgiven much love much." That's a powerful truth given to us by Jesus. How do you relate to that truth?

3. Some criticized Mary Magdalene for "wasting" her expensive gift as she worshiped Jesus, saying it was too extravagant. Do you think we can love Jesus too much? Why or why not?

4. How do you feel about Simon's response, who was uncomfortable with having a "sinner" like Mary enter his house? How comfortable are you with spending time with "sinners"? How comfortable are they with you? How can you create an environment of grace for people to meet Jesus in your home?

5

LOOKING AT THE FACE OF LOVE

(John)

JOHN 19:25-30

The death I was watching was killing me too.

When you see the person you love most in the world being crucified before your very eyes, it is enough to make you feel as though your own heart is nailed to a cross. Just a few feet from my tortured gaze, Jesus of Nazareth hung suspended, His death sentence being carried out one agonizing breath and drop of blood at a time. It was a sight that would be indelibly etched on my heart for the rest of my life.

Standing so close to the cross and being identified as a disciple of Jesus put me in jeopardy of signing my own death warrant. Being a follower of Jesus had never been popular, but standing at that moment between a mob insane with demonic hatred and a squadron of Roman soldiers with crucifixion on their agenda had lethal implications.

Still, thoughts of my own safety were the furthest thing from my mind. All the other disciples had fled into the darkness at Jesus' arrest the night before and were still hiding in the darkness of their own fear. But I stood at the foot of the cross, drawn there by my love for my Master. That love had led me to follow Jesus for more than three years. I could be no other place but near Him. Standing at the foot of the cross was the most dangerous place I could be, but it was the only place I wanted to be.

I was not standing there alone.

I was not the only one who loved Jesus, standing there at the foot of the cross . . .

not the only one with tears streaming down my face,
        not the only one whose heart was being pierced by the
        horrifying sight,
                not the only one whose love for Jesus overruled the
                urge of self-preservation.

Next to me, clutching each other in grief-stricken desperation, were Jesus' mother; Jesus' aunt Salome—my own mother; Mary Magdalene, whom Jesus had delivered from seven demons and a life of sin-filled destitution; and Mary the wife of Clopas. These women, too, had followed Jesus in life, and now they were willing to follow Him to death if need be. They were the only faces showing love for Jesus in the vast sea of people spread out before the cross. Most of the faces in the crowd were contorted by a mixture of twisted pleasure and hardened rebellion at the suffering they saw on the face of Jesus.

The face of Jesus was barely recognizable. I had seen that face at all times of the day, in nearly every conceivable situation, and I could never have imagined the way I saw it today. I had seen that face break into a huge smile with laughter as Jesus played with children or watched a lame man take his first steps after Jesus' healing touch. Sometimes, often at night by the flickering firelight, I had seen Jesus with a faraway look, as if He were looking into the future at things to come. I had seen that face strained by deep sorrow as Jesus had seen the effects of sin and death in the lives of people.

There were many times I saw Him moved with deep compassion as Jesus saw crowds of people harassed and helpless, like sheep without a shepherd. I had seen that face earnest and intense as Jesus taught those crowds Kingdom truths. There was the day I saw Jesus' face dark and magnificent in holy anger at the prideful stubbornness of religious hypocrites as He cleared the Temple of greedy merchants using God as a means to personal gain. So many times I had seen that face in prayer, so at home in conversation with His heavenly Father that it made me and the other disciples ask Jesus to teach us to pray like that too.

That wonderful face . . . with tears streaming down His cheeks and off His beard at the tomb of His friend Lazarus; strong and warrior-like, as He confronted demons and defeated them with the word of His authority; gentle and redemptive as He forgave the woman caught in the act of adultery; amused and delighted as He handed out the miraculous supply of loaves and fish to us who in turn fed 5,000 people from the lunch of one little boy; weary with exhaustion after seeing hundreds of people in a day, praying with them and touching them with His supernatural power; calm in the midst of a howling storm on the Sea of Galilee; in complete control as He ordered the waves to sit down and the wind to be still.

Up on a high mountain I had seen that face radiant, transformed with the glory of His majesty as He spoke to Moses and Elijah.

I had seen that face harden with courageous resolve as He told us about His impending death as we began our final journey to Jerusalem together.

Just last night, I had seen that face, so young in time and old in wisdom, in such agony that He was literally sweating great drops of blood in the Garden of Gethsemane . . . then saddened as Judas betrayed Him with a kiss on the cheek.

I had watched Him, regal and calm, as He faced His accusers, answering without reservation, "I AM," to the question of whether He, Jesus of Nazareth, was truly the Messiah, the Son of God.

Yes, I had grown to love that face; but now between the physical torture He was experiencing and the spiritual suffering He was enduring from the crushing weight of humanity's sin laid on Him, Jesus was barely recognizable.

At His trial, a mockery of Jewish justice, the priests who convicted Him of blasphemy for His fearless confirmation that He was the Messiah had blindfolded and beat that face over and over, spitting on Him while they pummeled Him. I recoiled in shock when I saw His lips broken and bleeding, His eyes blackened and swelling, His cheeks puffy from the blows. In their rage, supposedly motivated by righteous indignation, but in reality fueled by demonic instigation, the Pharisees pulled out patches of Jesus' beard, hurling their hatred in His face and pieces of His beard still attached to skin to the floor.

The punishment was only beginning.

The priests pushed, pulled and dragged Jesus on a journey that led them to Pilate, then to Herod and finally back to Pilate. They continued to beat Him along the way with words, fists and clubs, yet Jesus never once reciprocated with a look of hatred, vengeance, fear or

vindictiveness. The acuteness of His pain was obvious, but His serenity in the midst of the suffering was unmistakable.

When at last Pilate caved in to the demands and political threats
of the priests and the mob, the Roman soldiers went to work on Jesus
with their own form of torture, intentionally designed to bleed every bit
of life just short of death out of a condemned prisoner in order to make
death by crucifixion that much quicker. After all, they had better things
to do than sit around waiting for a condemned man to die. They led Jesus out into their courtyard where they first beat Him on the head with
a reed and, putting the reed in His hand as a mock scepter, they surrounded Him and jeered at Him with profane taunts. The mockery
was designed to strike at the heart of the prisoner's identity.

Then they went to work on His body.

Stripping Him naked, they bent Jesus over, tying His hands to a
pole, exposing Him to even more ridicule. Two soldiers, one on either
side, began systematically lashing Him with a despicable weapon
called the cat-o'-nine-tails. These were leather straps studded on the
ends with sharp bones and glass that would smash down on the prisoner's back and wrap around the trunk of his body, tearing flesh down
to the bone with every blow. The prisoner was literally beaten from
the ankles to the neck until blood spattered like rain on the soldiers
and the surrounding ground.

Some condemned men never made it past the flogging. Jesus did.
After the vicious whipping, the soldiers continued to mock Him in a
sadistic ritual they called "The King's Game." Finding a branch from
a thorn tree and gingerly fashioning the branch into a crown studded
with inch-long thorns, they slammed it down on His head, opening
even more wounds while mockingly paying Him homage as royalty.
Between the beatings of the priests, the lashes of the whip, the punc-
tures of the thorns and the finishing blows of the soldiers, the face of
Jesus was no longer recognizable as Jesus, and barely discernible as a
man. That was the face the women and crowd and I saw in front of us.

Several hours had passed since they had thrown Jesus down on
the ground on the splintered wood of the crosspiece and nailed Him
in place. As they lifted Jesus into the air, the crowd continued to pelt
Him with blasphemy and mockery. The soldiers, seemingly oblivious
to the eternal drama taking place in front of them, had gambled for

Jesus' robe, the last of His earthly possessions, and sat watching with cynical boredom.

The centurion began to look at Jesus with growing puzzlement and wonder as he heard Jesus hoarsely say, "Father, forgive them, for they know not what they do." He had *never* heard a plea for forgiveness from a prisoner on behalf of his executioners before. I could see that the more the centurion watched, the more he realized he had never seen *any* man die like this, and he had seen many.

The women continued to stand at the foot of the cross, crushed by their own pain and despair, crying tears of wrenching sorrow that seemed to come from the very depths of their heart. Instinctively I went over to my mother and Jesus' mother and put my arms around them, letting them lay their heads on my shoulders and wet my cloak with their tears. None of Jesus' brothers or sisters were there to comfort their mother, so I did. Over the years the families had known each other, and especially since I had become a disciple of Jesus, I grew to love Mary as much as my own mother. Joseph had been dead for some time. As the oldest son, Jesus had cared and provided for His mother even after He had left home to begin His journey culminating with His destiny at the cross. It was the responsibility of the oldest son to care for his mother if the father died and make sure that responsibility was covered in the event of his own death. For Jesus, the arrival of His own death would now be within minutes.

Jesus moved His head and winced as He put His full weight on His feet, pierced together and fastened onto the cross by a rusty spike. He pushed Himself up to capture a breath. The evil genius of crucifixion was that death came as a combination of massive blood loss, screaming physical agony and slow asphyxiation. Every breath was excruciatingly gained by forcing the body's weight on the spike driven through the feet, against and up the splinters of the cross high enough to allow air to rush into the lungs. Once gained, the crucified person could not release the breath until pushing himself up again. It was like breathing under water, gasping for air each time the man's head could break the surface, only infinitely more painful. Speaking only accentuated the torture. When the person no longer had the strength to capture a breath, death would soon follow. Of all the twisted ways men have invented to torture and kill, crucifixion is among the most hideous. It was all I could do to watch my beloved Friend and Lord suffer such a death.

Jesus turned His head again, and through swollen eyes He looked over at me and seemed to beckon me and His mother. The centurion stood aside in what must have been an unusual gesture of respect and let us come closer.

We were looking straight up at Him now, standing in the midst of the blood drops that had fallen to the ground. Even now, I can still remember the patterns the drops had made in the dust. Together, Mary the mother of the Messiah, and I, the disciple whom Jesus loved, stood gazing into that disfigured and yet divinely beautiful face. We could see the immense suffering in His eyes, yet we saw that familiar look of tender love we knew so well.

Jesus looked down at His mother, His love for her never more apparent. "Dear woman"—the term was a common one of endearment and respect—"here is your son." Then, turning to me, His voice showing His trust and love, He said, "Here is your mother." My arms around Mary, eyes full of tears, I looked up at Jesus and nodded. Yes. I would care for Mary as my own mother. To have Jesus trust me with such a responsibility was a privilege I would gladly take. Our eyes, Master and disciple, friend and friend, met in wordless, love-filled agreement.

It all came to me, then. Even in the midst of the agony of the cross, Jesus showed His love to those who loved Him most . . . and least.

It was that kind of love . . .

love that went beyond loving only those who loved Him,

loving the unlovely,

the unlovable

and the ones most resistant to His love . . .

It was that kind of love that had made me follow Jesus in the first place.

It was that kind of love that transformed me from a quick-to-anger "Son of Thunder" into the "Apostle of Love." It was the love I had seen on the face of Jesus day in and day out and now, finally, wholly evident on His face that led me to stand by that cross now. That love would carry me through the days and years ahead as I cared for Mary and countless others. The love of Jesus crucified selfishness in me and filled me with an overflow of His unconditional love.

It is the same love that comes to all who will stand at the foot of the cross, look up into that matchless face of love and accept gladly whatever Jesus asks us to do. It is only at the cross that we can truly see the Savior's face of love—only at the cross that we can truly receive His heart of love.

Come. Stand with me at the foot of the cross. Look at the face of love. Listen to the voice of love. Open your life to the King of love.

In Jesus, find the love that will change you forever.

BEYOND THE STORY
To Help You Think, Pray, Share and Do

1. John is referred to as "the disciple whom Jesus loved." He was one of the inner circle of three disciples who were especially close to the Lord. The opening line of this story is "The death I was watching was killing me too." Have you had the experience of losing someone you loved? How can you relate to John's feelings?

2. This story especially focuses on the face of Jesus, which has been characterized by artists and authors in many ways down through the centuries. How do you envision the face of Jesus? Why?

3. Jesus trusted John with the care of His mother—a sacred responsibility. If someone you knew asked you to take over care for a family member of theirs because they were dying, how would you respond?

4. John testifies at the end of this story that the love of Jesus transformed his life from the inside out. How has Jesus changed your life?

6

Arms Open Wide
(Peter)

Luke 22:39-53

His arms were open wide again.

Standing far back at the edge of the seething mass of people witnessing a crucifixion, trying to stay unnoticed, those open arms were about all Peter could see. The face and other features of Jesus were blurred by distance and increasing darkness, but Peter could see those arms open wide in wounded agony.

He desperately wanted to be closer, but shame and fear had created a chasm far greater than that caused by the crowd. He was alienated and alone at the edge of the chaos, drawn by his love for Jesus and repelled by his terror at what might happen if he was recognized again by his connection to the man on the middle cross. He had betrayed his Master when He needed him most, and his self-confident assertions that he would never let Jesus down had only amplified the humiliation of his collapse.

His failure last night had been one of several breakdowns in recent days that revealed Peter's deficiencies beneath his verbal declarations. Three years of apprenticeship with Jesus and ministry successes had made him feel that he had moved beyond the need to worry about personal failure. Why worry when you walked so close to the Son of God? After all, he was one of the inner circle of three among the chosen 12, wasn't he? Living close to Jesus can make a man feel invincible if he's not careful, and Peter wasn't a man known for being careful.

Things had been going so well . . . Jesus' popularity had grown immensely across the land in spite of the intensifying opposition from the religious leaders of their nation. Being recognized as a member of Jesus' team brought a level of recognition that Peter enjoyed and fed a need for more. Increasing calls for Jesus to take a position of national leadership both spiritually and politically was pretty heady stuff. Peter's personality lent itself to a need for recognition and a desire to be in front of people. He had become the spokesman for the group of 12 disciples and relished his place as a close confidant of Christ.

Then, as if recognizing a countdown had begun, a shift took place in Jesus' attitude and actions.

They were in Caesarea Philippi in northern Galilee, talking about their day around an evening fire, the flickering light dancing across their features, when Jesus had looked around the circle and asked, "Who do people say that the Son of Man is?" Different disciples contributed misconceptions and fabrications about Jesus generated by various sectors of their society. Prophet . . . resurrected historical hero . . . political opportunist . . . great teacher . . . healer . . . popular champion of common folks, nemesis of religious leaders with fancy clothes and empty hearts . . . demon-possessed lunatic . . . spiritual fraud . . . the opinions about Jesus spanned the spectrum.

Then Jesus leaned in and looked intently around the circle of His disciples. "But you . . . who do *you* say I am?" Peter had answered abruptly, straight from his heart, "You are the Messiah, the Son of the Living God!" Jesus nodded approvingly, and told Peter that his answer was based on revelation from His Father in heaven. Further, He'd told Peter that he would be a keystone (Petros) as Jesus built His church on the rock-solid foundation He Himself would be (Petra). Peter and others would be given Kingdom keys to use His authority to release or restrict things in the spiritual realm. Peter could barely contain his pleasure and pride at being so honored. He'd answered correctly and would be rewarded handsomely! Peter was a key man in the Kingdom!

Jesus paused, and then reminded them again of a reality they had not wanted to hear, speaking solemnly. He was going to Jerusalem, not to take his place as messianic ruler over the hated Romans and God's Temple, but to suffer and die at the hands of the very people who prayed regularly for His coming!

When he heard that, Peter sat in stupefied bewilderment. This did not make sense . . . Jesus was the Messiah . . . the King! He was going to rule, and Peter would be one of His key leaders! The way to victory was not by descending to death; it was by ascending to supremacy!

Peter had taken Jesus aside to try to correct Him. "No, Lord! This will never happen to You. I won't let it! You've got it all wrong."

Jesus' rebuke was sharp and stinging as He turned His back on Peter. "Get behind me, Satan! You are a stumbling block to me because you are not thinking about God's perspective, only your own."

Peter had retreated dumbly, staggering back to his sleeping place at the outside shadows of the fire. Nothing more was said that night. He had blustered his way into another blunder, but this time Jesus' response had left him puzzled and humbled.

Not long after that Jesus had taken Peter, James and John with Him to the top of Mount Hermon. It was reassuring to Peter to be included in the inner circle again. Jesus had acted as if He had forgotten his gaffe and all was forgiven. At the summit they saw His divine glory shining through His physical body, and Jesus spoke with Elijah and Moses about His upcoming journey to the cross. It was a sacred, spectacular moment that the three men would forever recount with awe. Majesty on the mountaintop captivated them.

Peter again rushed to insert his plan to make things better as he suggested they build little booths as shrines for Christ and Moses and Elijah so people could have the same mountaintop experience they were having. Suddenly the entire mountaintop was enveloped by the awesome, shining, weighty Presence of God Himself, and they heard a Voice speak: "This is My beloved Son. I take delight in Him. Listen to Him!" Again, Peter felt like he'd messed up, and this time the Almighty Himself had reprimanded him. His misunderstanding of God's plans, his misinformed attempts to add his ideas to God's agenda and his mixed motives to inflate his own importance were painfully exposed.

They'd arrived in Jerusalem . . . they had entered to a huge crowd with great fanfare and adulation. Perhaps there was yet hope for Peter's aspirations to be achieved. Then the Passover Seder meal in an upper room . . . Peter had stuck his foot in his mouth again when Jesus began to wash the disciples' feet like a servant . . . unheard of for the master of a feast. When he had protested that Jesus would never wash *his* feet, the Lord just looked at him with a hint of disappointment and told him that if He didn't wash Peter's feet, then Peter really didn't belong to Him at all. This was the very example the Lord wanted them to emulate—to lead by serving. Peter leaned back, talking to himself. *Why can't you keep your big mouth shut?* he fumed. *It doesn't seem like I can do anything right.*

The meal began with the easy familiarity of tradition, but then came Jesus' shocking announcement that one of them would betray Jesus and they'd all scatter in fear. Around the room the disciples were stunned and spontaneously asked, "It's not me, is it, Lord?" Answering so that only John who was leaning back toward His chest could hear, Jesus had told them that the one with whom He shared a morsel He dipped in the bowl was the betrayer. Peter, sitting at the end of the table, leaned forward and asked John with his eyes who the betrayer was. John looked over at Judas with an almost imperceptible nod toward him. When Jesus handed the piece of bread to Judas, Peter instinctively started to rise from his place, a low growl in his throat. No one would betray His Master while Peter was there to protect Him! Jesus put up His hand with a warning look to stop him and Peter sat down reluctantly as Jesus told Judas to do what he had to do. Judas had left the upper room with Peter's eyes blazing anger after him. Leaning back toward Jesus, he asserted with his typical bravado, "Even if everyone runs away, I never will! I will never deny You. I'm ready to die for You!"

Jesus turned so that He could look Peter full in the face and said nothing for a long moment. He continued to look at Peter patiently, with a hint of pity. "Simon . . . Simon," Jesus said with deep feeling, calling him by his given name. "Satan has asked me if he can have you to sift you as wheat. He's going to find out what you are really made of. But I have prayed for you that your faith will not fail."

Peter protested, his eyes pleading, "Lord, I'm ready to go to prison for You. I'd die for You!"

Jesus shook His head slightly and put His hand on Peter's shoulder. "Before the rooster crows twice this night, you will deny me three times. But when you turn back, strengthen your brothers."

Again Peter felt like he'd failed a test at the level of both his commitment to Christ and his character. How could things possibly go so downhill in such a short period of time?

They'd gone to the garden at the olive presses of Gethsemane where Jesus had asked the three to watch and pray with Him. He'd gone ahead to an open space where the moonlight shone on a large flat rock and knelt there, then spread Himself facedown on it. At first they had listened to his anguished conversation with His heavenly Father and sensed how alone their Master felt as He willingly surrendered to His Father's will. The day had been so long . . . it was late into the night already . . . so much had happened to try to comprehend . . . and before they knew it, Peter and his companions' heavy eyelids closed, their heads sunk down to their chests, fast asleep.

It felt like they had just nodded off when Jesus shook them awake. His hair was wet with perspiration, His eyes red with tears and His face streaked with rivulets of sweaty blood. Disappointment showed in His eyes as He leaned down to look at them. "Why are you sleeping when I needed you to pray with me?" He said. "Couldn't you even stay awake one hour?" Then His look turned to understanding as He said, "I know . . . the spirit is willing but the flesh is weak. Men, you've got to stay awake and pray so you won't fall into temptation." Once again Peter had let Jesus down, and he felt embarrassment and a growing desire to rectify his disappointing behavior.

Then, looking up at the sound of approaching footsteps, the rumble of hushed eager voices and dozens of lanterns swinging in the night, Jesus said, "It's time. Get up . . . my betrayer is coming."

They stood to meet the rabble of Temple guards, Roman soldiers and low level priests . . . watched Judas brazenly greet Jesus with a kiss . . . saw the mob fall back in fear as Jesus identified Himself, expecting Him to use some of the supernatural power they'd heard so much about . . . gaped with stunned apprehension as soldiers stepped forward to arrest Him . . .

Here was Peter's chance to show Jesus that he was worthy of His trust again! Reaching under his cloak, he drew a short sword, stepped forward with a roaring "NO!" and swung wildly at the nearest apprehender. He would take the head off the first person who tried to take his Master!

He missed. His impulsive blow bypassed all the soldiers and banged off the side of the head of an unarmed man, taking his ear off. The man, who Peter recognized as Malchus, a slave of the high priest, dropped to the ground in a shriek of agony. Instantly the scraping sounds of dozens of swords being unsheathed brought a sudden deadly tension to the scene. One wrong move and the garden would be slippery with blood.

Jesus took command, defusing the explosive situation. He knelt down before Malchus, gently placing His hands on both sides of his head. When He pulled them back, Malchus reached a bloody hand to find his ear reattached and the pain completely gone. Then Jesus looked up at Peter and said, "Put your sword away! Enough of this! If you live by the sword, you'll die by it too. Don't you know I could call My Father and He'd send me more than twelve legions of angels to my defense? No . . . it's got to happen this way as the Scriptures say."

Peter's attempt at assistance had been an abysmal failure. The soldiers stepped forward, swords drawn, with priests behind them eagerly grasping clubs ready to release their pent-up anger on anyone identified with the Nazarene. The last vestige of courage evaporated and the disciples ran in panicked terror.

He ran with the rest of the disciples as they scattered in all directions, fearing for their lives, expecting at any moment to be caught from behind and dragged down or run through. After he sprinted through the tangled maze of olive branches, he pulled up short, his breath coming in ragged gasps, heart pounding fueled by adrenaline and panic. Then, in alarmed realization that his Master had been arrested by a rabble of Temple guards and priests with low-level positions and upper-echelon ambitions, he turned back.

Covering his face to obscure his features, he worked his way back to a courtyard where people waited while Jesus began His appearances before religious leaders who had already predetermined His fate. He stood around a fire, warming his hands, straining to hear any scrap of information. It was in the midst of that crowd that he denied knowing Jesus not once, but three distinct times. The first betrayal had been shruggingly benign as a servant approached him with an inquisitive, "Weren't you with the Galilean too?" He'd put up his hands and backed away in mock disbelief. "I don't know what you're talking about," he said.

He edged closer to the gateway where the trial would be held, trying to see inside without being seen. It didn't work. Another woman walked up to him, peering as if trying to recall where she had seen him before. Then, recognition dawning on her face, she pointed at him accusingly and loudly declared, "This man was with Jesus the Nazarene! He's one of His followers!" Peter had shaken his head violently and emphatically, his voice strained and angry as he pointed back at her. "As the Almighty is my witness, I don't know the man!" He moved back further into the shadows, trying to make himself undetectable.

His third betrayal was staggeringly brazen. He tried to blend in with the crowd, joining the small talk as if he belonged there. Someone walked over and said, "You've got to be one of those Jesus followers . . . your accent gives you away." He had reacted like a cornered animal. Others pulled back in shock by the wild look in his eyes and the snarling words spewing from his mouth—profane curses he hadn't used for years. He panicked, his terrified mind dredging up ugly, dirty words that had been hiding in the recesses of his heart as he tried to protect himself at any cost. His shocking reaction denied and then denounced any affiliation with Jesus.

It was at that moment—a moment he would never again remember without regret and shame; a perfect storm of a moment when all the consequences of his denials converged and imploded on him— that a rooster crowed twice as if for emphasis and Peter looked up to meet the eyes of Jesus as soldiers brusquely pushed Him past Peter and the crowd through the gateway and into the meeting place. The prophecy of Jesus about this moment was being played out in real time. On Peter's face, horrified comprehension. On Jesus' face, knowing compassion.

He had run again, this time to an isolated place where he collapsed into a heap of bitter, scalding tears that wracked his body with remorse. He wept until the tears were gone; but the shame and ache of his betrayal wouldn't go away. He'd failed every opportunity to show his loyalty to Christ, and his final public downfall was a complete collapse for all to see. For a long time he lay on the ground, his big hands clenching and unclenching, not sure what to do. What could he do? Dumbly he pulled himself to his feet, covered his face so that he couldn't be recognized and stumbled in the direction of a howling mob gathered for Golgotha.

Now the big fisherman stood as far away as he could and still see Jesus . . . and he wondered how he could have gone so wrong when he thought he was so strong.

His Master's arms were open wide again . . .

Those big strong arms, hardened and sinewy from long hours working with stone, wood and tools. His forearms were larger than most men's, muscles swelled by gripping hammer, chisel and saw. His hands were calloused like many who supported their families with the sweat of sustained effort. His fingers had seen their share of cuts and cracked nails from constant use.

Now He was using nails and wood in a way that only He could have ever imagined.

The first time Peter had seen those arms open wide was in welcoming acceptance. His brother, Andrew, had been talking constantly about a rabbi he'd met down along the Jordan River. For the normally quiet Andrew, to talk much about anything was out of character. In fact, Peter, known to his friends and family as Simon, was the one renowned for his gift of gab. But Simon had actually noticed a difference in Andrew's character since he'd met Jesus of Nazareth, and it intrigued him. Religious fads and fakes came and went, easily dismissed as far as he was concerned. But real life change . . . that was something else. Still, Simon stayed on shore or aboard ship, sticking to what he knew best, seeking the shiny, slimy source of his livelihood.

Then one day, Andrew's Rabbi appeared on *his* shore and asked to use *his* ship. Jesus backed up memorable teaching with a tip that led to a miraculous catch, and Peter was hooked. Prideful bravado crumbled into humble repentance as he fell at Jesus' feet, and those arms opened wide in welcoming acceptance. Jesus' eyes sparkled and His face broke into a huge smile as strong hands reached out to pull Peter onto his feet and into a welcoming embrace of forgiveness and friendship. That was the day Peter gained new reasons to live. Andrew's Rabbi became his Master and he became a fisher of souls. It was a decision he never regretted.

He'd seen those arms open wide in welcoming acceptance so many times to so many kinds of people over the three years he'd followed Jesus . . . in stark contrast to other religious leaders. Their arms were usually folded tightly across their chests in prideful judgment or protection lest they be contaminated by unclean, undeserving, spiritually deficient people. For Jesus, it seemed that the greater the need and religious unacceptability, the more He'd open wide those arms.

A parade of memories passed through Peter's mind—so many people had been welcomed by those open arms . . .

. . . a woman Jesus healed after 12 years of bleeding that repulsed others. Jesus received her with open arms, hugging her to His heart like a father welcoming a daughter returning home after being away for too long . . .

. . . working folks the wealthy never noticed . . .

. . . wealthy people who were outwardly affluent but inwardly impoverished . . . the people who looked like they had it all outwardly but lived with yearning need inwardly . . .

. . . children everywhere went eagerly to have those big, strong arms toss them on His shoulder as laughter filled the air . . .

. . . holding Martha and Mary close as they wept after the temporary death of their brother, Lazarus . . .

. . . standing before thousands of people on a hillside just up from the rocky shore of the Sea of Galilee, inviting people to experience the power of God for their needs . . .

Those wide-open arms welcoming people back home to God. Peter had seen thousands run to that redemptive embrace. He'd seen those arms opened wide and extended to heaven in worship.

His followers had seen Him at prescribed times of prayer, regular Sabbath meetings at their local synagogues—all the times when a person would expect religious behavior. When Jesus would open those arms wide to heaven, religious rituals became infused with the supernatural joy of a relationship with God.

Often the disciples had gazed in wonder as Jesus would stop in the midst of an ordinary event and turn it into an opportunity for extraordinary connection with His Father. All of life was sacred. Every moment was to be savored as a gift from above. Flowers along the way . . . children who just wanted to grab Jesus' leg and play . . . to embrace someone in a hug that seemed to envelop them in the arms of God. It was so natural for Jesus to stop and open His arms wide in gratitude and adoration. It was, in fact, supernaturally natural. It fed a longing in Peter and the disciples to have that kind of familial familiarity with the Father too.

Now he was looking at those arms open wide, fastened by love to a cross. He longed to run to the cross and join John and the others who were standing there for Him. But the distance was too great. The chasm caused by his collapse and betrayal was so vast that he felt he'd never be able to get close to Jesus again. He'd been taken down by his own divided heart.

He couldn't hear anything being said by Jesus and those around the cross; he wouldn't allow himself to get that close . . . until he heard one word shouted by that familiar Voice . . . "Finished!"

Jesus had accomplished His mission, just as He had told them He would. Those arms open wide were now an eternal invitation to all who wanted to come home to God. If they came to Him through those wide-open arms of sacrificial love, anyone and everyone was welcome.

It all made sense then. As if it came to him from a great distance, a ray of hope began to dawn in Peter's heart. If He was finished, then maybe Peter wasn't.

Those arms open wide could still welcome Peter home. Hadn't Jesus said that when Peter came back he was to strengthen his brothers?

He turned to go; he'd find the others. They'd wait like Jesus had told them, like He'd promised when He said He'd send another Comforter. Peter knew he'd see those arms open wide again . . . for him.

When the pressure's on, the true nature of our character surfaces, often exposing a divided heart struggling with who is truly ruling on the throne of our life. Peter is not the first follower of Jesus to fail miserably because he reserved the right to tell the Lord how to run things. What makes sense in the natural realm, especially in helping us ascend to the power and popularity we desire so that we can look good, is completely bankrupt in the supernatural realm. It would take the cleansing and filling of the Holy Spirit at Pentecost to give Peter the undivided heart he needed to take the Master's message beyond his borders and boundaries for those who wanted Him, too.

In our shame, we often run away like Peter, isolating ourselves from opportunities to hear the Lord speak again to us and restore us to a relationship with Him. We remove ourselves from fellowship with other believers; we withdraw from worship; we close our hearts to the Word. We're afraid, ashamed and perhaps a bit too defiant to allow ourselves to get close enough to hear. We stand at the edge of the crowd with others who feel far from God too.

It's at those times—when we're too far away to hear—that all we need to do is lift our eyes to see those arms open wide. They invite us, welcome us back. If you can't hear His voice, all you have to do is see His arms open wide . . . for you.

BEYOND THE STORY
To Help You Think, Pray, Share and Do

1. Peter stumbled and fell because he felt he was so close to Christ that he was immune to temptation and failure. How can you relate to that? What lessons can you learn from Peter's story?

2. After he denied the Lord, Peter felt so ashamed that he didn't want to come near to Christ again. Many people experience similar feelings and stay away from the Lord. How does the picture of "His arms open wide" speak to you?

3. Ultimately, Peter was restored and became a powerful force for Christ. How does this speak to you about restoring leaders (who have fallen) back into places of spiritual leadership?

4. Do you know someone who had been effective in ministry but is now out of spiritual leadership? How can you pray for them . . . reach out to them . . . encourage them? Be intentional about doing that this coming week.

7

THE UNSEEN ONES
(Hosts of Angels and Hordes of Demons)

MATTHEW 26:53

With one word they could end all this.

Two massive supernatural armies faced each other far above the eternal drama taking place below them . . . visible only to each other.

The chasm separating them was as infinite and definite as heaven and hell.

On one side the host of heaven; on the other side the hordes of hell.

The hordes jeered and roared with fiendish triumph, gloating with demonic glee. Swarming, snarling, shouting, sniveling, they concentrated all their hated on the man on the middle cross. Like a dark, boiling cloud, the demons thronged around Him, haranguing, harassing, clawing. What human hands, whips and nails had done to His body over the past hours, they were now intensifying as they released pent-up ages of frustration on Him. Voices of individual demons were indistinguishable as multiplied shrieks, howls, growls and screams all blended into an ugly, buzzing cacophony of sound, one word seeming to emerge from the many . . .

"Death . . . death . . . death . . ."

The man on the middle cross ignored them, concentrating all His attention on finishing His mission.

The demons appeared to act as if they didn't notice the vast multitudes of heavenly warriors that outnumbered them two to one, although in the midst of their sulfurous celebration they kept glancing toward the angels, nervously wondering why they remained disengaged and inactive. It was unlike the host of heaven to not decisively move to countermand the activities of the horde, and it puzzled them.

Across the chasm, tension and pent-up anguish resonated through the angelic ranks. The strain of holding back when they yearned for action was palpable. Normally radiant with the reflected brilliance of heaven, their luminescence was muted and dim. The gathering darkness below them and above them was both natural and super-natural. It was if the doorway to heaven were closing, separating them from the divine energy and vitality of the Almighty. At the same time, it seemed that the doorway of the depths of hell had been flung open, spewing tangible darkness and every vile essence imagi-nable. They'd never experienced anything like it before and it made them uneasy.

At the head of the immense army, spread out and lined up in bat-tle formation, two angelic generals conferred.

"With one word we could end all this . . . why doesn't He give it?" The strain in Gabriel's voice was plain. "Why doesn't the Father say something? Why doesn't the Son call us to help Him? He told the mob that arrested Him in the garden that with one word He could com-mand twelve legions of us to His aid. Why are we being held back? With just one word—" His hand gripped his sword, clenching and un-clenching it in his urgency to use it.

Michael's response showed his heaviness as well. "Gabriel, I know you are the Almighty's greatest messenger, and this is one message you would love to deliver. But you and I both know the Father's ex-plicit instructions. We cannot, we must not help or interfere in any way. As the prince responsible for Israel, this is my greatest nightmare come to pass. God's chosen people are rejecting the very one sent to be their Messiah."

Gabriel nodded soberly. "You are right. I know it. We are His mes-sengers, His ministers to serve His saints, His mighty warriors to pro-tect His people and inflict His punishment so the Almighty's mission can be accomplished on earth. But this is one mission the Son must accomplish alone."

Michael finished for him. "And until He does, this is the hour that darkness reigns."

Gabriel looked beyond the city of Jerusalem to the ridges of Beth-lehem a few miles away. "It was only a little over 33 earthly years ago that we were guarding Him and His parents as He was born in Bethlehem. What a night that was! God the Son incarnate, come to make His home with them so they could one day make their home with Him. Never before had the choir around the throne of the Father been allowed to sing to earthly beings like that—simple shepherds though they were. It did make sense, though. Everything our Lord does makes perfect sense. How perfect that the shepherds protecting sheep for the sacrifices in the Temple would be among the first to welcome and worship the Lamb of God who would be slain for the sins of the whole world."

Michael nodded. "How the Father, Son and Spirit love these frail creatures created in Their image! How tenderly He cares for them, how generously He provides for them! How powerfully He acts on their behalf! How graciously He calls them to come home to His heart even after they've separated themselves from Him with their own sinful choices. What an honor it is to serve Him . . . and them."

Michael's and Gabriel's service had covered centuries of human time . . . had been glory and delight from the dawn of creation and the conception of humans crafted in the Lord's image when His Spirit breathed life into them. That creation had been forever altered and intensified when Lucifer, one of the highest among them, had been infected with a desire to ascend to God's throne and take His place. His own pride and ambition had in turn contaminated those under his leadership until he attempted a full-scale rebellion against the Almighty. His coup was quickly and decisively smashed, his sentence delivered swiftly.

Lucifer and a third of the angels were expelled from heaven, allowed to exist but forever under the condemnation of God. With their expulsion from the perfection of heaven and the presence of God, they became everything heaven was not. Selfishness putrefied them from the inside out. They sought darkness rather than light, raw power instead of reverent service, sin instead of holy love. Lucifer—originally named "Morning Star," became known by many other names that now matched his true character: Satan . . . Slanderer . . . Accuser . . . Adversary. He assumed the title of "prince of this world," though he ruled nothing. The angels that had shared the nature as servants of God now became demons whose nature was distorted by servitude to Satan and secret designs to take the Father's place. They had become

masters at taking every good gift the Father had designed and twist-
ing them with half-truths until what God intended for purity, pleasure and provision became distorted, destructive and deadly.

Lucifer had worked his evil insinuations on Eve and then leveraged her assent to accomplish his intentions with Adam as well. He
promised them divine knowledge—godlikeness. His real intention was
to turn their intent to worship and obey the Father—what had come
so naturally from pure hearts—to now be given to him. His ultimate
deception was to make them think they were now in control of their
lives, rulers of their own hearts. What the humans didn't know is that
every selfish attitude and action was a reflection of worship to Lucifer;
being worshiped as if *he* was God was his ultimate goal.

Now sin had infected the human race; but unlike the angels, they
had the opportunity and possibility to be redeemed and restored
again to a right relationship with the Father. The battle for the souls
of men and women—they that mattered most to God—became a
fierce contest of each individual's choices within and spiritual influences without.

The demons emulating Lucifer continued his strategy of intimi-
dation by insinuation, suggestion and accusation. They really had little power, for even their actions were limited by God; they could only
do what they did at the end of a divine leash. Yet, they were allowed to
use the power of the lie with devastating effects. Individual choices
influenced family environments. Family upbringings influenced community downfalls. Communities blended together to form cultures
that identified entire nations and regions of the world. Kingdoms rose
and fell as battles waged to influence them.

Angels and demons each had their assignments over people, families, communities and nations. The angels worked on the Father's behalf, carrying out His orders without violating the free will of the
humans. Generations and centuries of Luciferic lies competing with
God's redemptive truths repeated themselves in the lives of individuals. From hell's point of view, this cycle would continue indefinitely.
It became a key doctrine they fleshed out in various religions—that
there would be no final accounting for a person's actions, no ultimate
justice, no real certainty of a person's condition spiritually as each human tried to work off his or her load of sin and guilt and grief.

As long as these dark forces could keep people focused on themselves with selfishness as their main motivation, things would be all right. If they ever acknowledged God's ultimate justice and judgment, they knew people would have to get serious about it. If hell ever acknowledged it, Satan and his demons knew their condemnation would be complete and their judgment final.

So, they did everything they could to distort eternal realities and verities. Focusing on temporal, selfish inclinations nourished demonic needs. Demons even allowed humans to think they would share their dark power with them, developing myriads of magic incantations people thought controlled demonic power but in reality were invocations of demonic praise. Only too late did deceived people realize that the demons they thought they controlled had actually been manipulating them all along. At the moment of death came reality, and for those who had chosen the dark way of selfishness, it was too late.

Death brought the temporal decisions people made during their physical life to a definitive eternal destiny. Death revealed if they had chosen to live under God's reign, or wanted to remain separated from Him by their decision to rule their own lives. However, God's decision was the final summation of their eternal destination. While the destination of the fallen angels had been decided and was irrevocable, while humans lived, they had the opportunity to use the gift of free will to accept God's gracious invitation to relationship with Him, reestablished on earth and continued in heaven.

Both angels and demons were doing everything they could to help influence those eternal decisions made by humans. Both the righteous dead and the unrighteous dead went to a place many humans called Hades—a shadowy place suspended between heaven and hell, a cosmic waiting room. A great chasm separated them, although they could see each other. What happened there didn't affect their destiny. It was a place where God had designated they would wait until an event He had determined from the foundation of the world would finally open the entrance to the final destinations of either heaven or hell. Then Hades would no longer be needed.

The angels knew the Lord God had an eternal plan. They didn't completely understand it—there were things regarding the salvation of humans that they longed to look into but couldn't fully comprehend or begin to experience themselves. Though they were supernatural beings, they were still lower in the divine order than the creature created in God's own image. They delivered God's messages and mandates but could not be delivered and saved like men and women. The closest they could get was to rejoice when they saw one sinner repent and find his or her way back to the Father. That salvation song that only humans could sing and angels could celebrate was some of the sweetest music heard in heaven.

Now the spiritual struggles of the ages, unfolding according to the Father's plan, had come to a climax with the Son finishing His mission on the cross. Satan and his demons saw it as their chance to defeat and unseat the Son so they could assume a place of spiritual ascendancy, blinded by their selfish audacity. The Father would use the perfect sacrifice of His Son to redeem humanity for all eternity and seal the destiny of sin, death, hell and Satan with His ultimate certainty.

Gabriel, Michael and the host of heaven watched, wept and waited—those six hours of human time seeming like an eternity as the Son of God suffered in isolation. He wasn't alone. The demonic horde spewed their putrid bile; the human mob shook their fists and added their unwitting vile taunts and threats. Soldiers sat on their haunches throwing dice as they divided up the spoils of condemned men, unmindful of the eternal drama playing out in front of them. Only His mother and a handful of others stood weeping near the foot of the cross, allowed close by a sympathetic Roman centurion.

And the angels were silent, held back by divine command until the mission was done. Only once had they been allowed to assist in any way since the Master and His men had finished the Passover meal the night before. In the Garden, as Jesus had agonized in prayer, His humanness pleading with the Father to find another way than the anguish ahead of Him, Gabriel had been allowed to appear and strengthen Him, reminding Him again of His identity as King of the Universe and Savior of the world. Gabriel's physical and spiritual encouragement had been welcome because Jesus' human companions had fallen asleep when He most needed their support. Gabriel stood guard as the Son finished His tearful conversation with the Father, the eternal plan agreed upon one more time: "Nevertheless, not My will but Yours be done."

When Judas arrived, Gabriel instinctively knew that Lucifer was controlling him, and he started to move forward to meet the threat. It was at that moment that the Father stopped him, and with him the entire angelic contingent of warriors. Nearly 72,000 of them were waiting for a word to dispatch the hundreds of human arrestors at the scene; and innumerable angelic legions more were available. When Jesus said, "This must happen so the Scripture might be fulfilled . . . this is the hour when darkness has dominion," He was speaking to them as well as to the earthly beings.

So they had withdrawn, never far away but staying separate as they watched the events unfold. Six human trials, monstrously unjust, yet allowed and mandated by Divine justice. Verbal, physical, emotional and spiritual assault pounded Jesus in every way from every dimension, and He bore it with regal calm in spite of His immense pain. Then, finally, the cross. All of heaven's hosts and all of hell's hordes gathered as never before in all eternity.

They listened as Jesus spoke, every word fulfilling Scripture and significant to those He shared His heart with. They leaned in to hear a prayer for forgiveness for those who had rejected and crucified Him; the promise of paradise for a penitent thief; tenderness as He transferred care for His mother to John.

The sun stopped shining as if creation itself couldn't bear to watch what was happening to its Creator, and then the darkness deepened as if every shred of divine presence had been withdrawn. Jesus looked up, His voice anguished. "*Eloi, Eloi, lama sabachthani*—My God, My God, why have *You* forsaken Me?" With those words, the sound of angels groaning in grief rippled through their ranks. Never before had the Father, Son and Spirit ever been separated! Their joyous, perfect trinity of unity and harmony was the source of all the melody of heaven and earth. Their desire to share that relationship with humanity was Their goal; and now the Trinity was incomplete as Father turned His back on His Son, who bore and became sin for every human who would ever live. Holiness rejecting sin. Purity staying pure. Love going to an infinite degree for justice to be done—where grace and truth could still coexist in reality. The penalty for sin becoming the barrier between Father and Son.

Gabriel leaned forward intently. "Listen," he said, his voice hushed. First one, then another, then another—when they would have least expected it and should have most anticipated it . . . the salvation song! The thief hanging next to Jesus . . . the centurion looking up at Him in humble awe . . . they were deciding! Their hearts were singing the song of the saved! The host of heaven leaned in to listen, tears of joy streaming down their faces as comprehension began to dawn.

The demonic horde surged in a greater frenzy, believing Jesus' end was near, not realizing that the end would be theirs.

It was 3:00 in the afternoon now—the Passover lamb was being sacrificed in the Temple, its blood spilling out to symbolically cleanse sin.

The Lamb of God threw back His head and shouted so all of heaven, earth and hell could hear.

"It is finished!"

The words reverberated through the seen and unseen world, their effect instantly noticeable.

With Jesus' shout of victory, the demonic horde was suddenly shocked into silence and they began to tremble. This was not what they had expected! This was a declaration of triumph, not a whimper of defeat! Jesus had taken their plan to defeat Him and turned it back on them, shattering their satanic schemes in a stunning sovereign statement. By His death, Jesus had killed death! In bearing sin, He had forever broken its power! In allowing hell and its hordes to "defeat" Him, He had forever conquered them and confirmed their condemnation. The Son's mission was accomplished; the Trinity's plan to redeem and restore creation was achieved.

The host of heaven roared their affirmation. Now they understood! Supernatural illumination suddenly burst from above, below and around them, and they radiated and reflected the Glory now restored!

Jesus smiled, His mission accomplished. He looked up, the Trinity relationship now feeling reconnected, never to sense separation again. "Father," He said, "into Your hands I commit My spirit . . ."

And with that, Jesus left His broken, bleeding body behind, His spirit stepping out in redemptive radiance.

Above them, Gabriel and Michael heard the Father speak. "Now," He said, and that one word was all it took.

Instantly the host of heaven sprang into fierce, joyous action, descending on the demonic hoard with holy fury, releasing their wrath on the unclean spirits who had tormented their Master. Now it was their turn! Demons scattered as angelic warriors inflicted punishment on them with supernatural intensity. Satan ran for cover; what he had intended to be his moment of triumph became his greatest moment of terror. In both the natural and the supernatural realm, light once again reigned.

Michael and Gabriel sped to Jesus' side, bowing before Him in awe and adoration, overwhelmed by what He had just done to accomplish salvation. It occurred to them that every knee would bow to Jesus, King of kings, Lord of lords! The host returned from dispelling the demons, and millions upon millions of them knelt in worship with Michael and Gabriel—an angelic army shimmering in heavenly, joyous, resplendent majesty as far as any eye could see!

Jesus smiled at them as He acknowledged their worship. "Come," He said, "we have another place to visit." Assigning some of the warriors to guard Jesus' body as His mother and some others lovingly retrieved it from the cross and took it to a tomb nearby—a duty they would solemnly fulfill until Sunday morning—Gabriel, Michael and the rest of the host followed Jesus.

Their destination: Hades.

Arriving there, the shadows fled before the light of the presence of Christ. Stepping into the great chasm between the righteous and the unrighteous dead, He proclaimed what He had just done for salvation to be accomplished and the entrances to heaven and hell to be unsealed. No longer would Hades be needed. With His mission completed, death's door would now lead immediately to eternal residence in heaven or hell.

Gabriel, Michael and the heavenly host watched in admiration, shining in delight as they listened to Jesus preach. The righteous dead flocked to Christ, realizing that He was the one they'd been waiting for to open the door to heaven. The unrighteous dead recoiled in horror, realizing who they had rejected and the consequences of their choices. The door of hell opened below them and they disappeared into its fiery, horrific darkness. Hades evaporated until all that remained was the King, His warriors and His redeemed bathed in the brilliance of salvation splendor.

The Son of God stood there at the center of it, the righteous dead surrounding Him in reverent awe, now kneeling in adoration with the angels. They were free to follow Him to heaven. The price had been paid. Their faith had been fulfilled. His victory over sin, death and hell was now their victory, too. Their longing for fellowship with their Father Creator would forever be realized.

Jesus turned to Gabriel and Michael and smiled. "Let's go home," He said.

They did, accompanying the Son and the saved as the heavenly honor guard they were. The Son's mission was finished; they would continue to carry on theirs. History would be forever marked and measured by what Christ had accomplished on the cross. An empty tomb and His resurrected body would forever confirm His victory until final Judgment Day. Their angelic ministry would continue, as would the work of their demonic opponents; but the Host knew that one day they'd be coming back with the King . . .

not to witness His crucifixion on earth,

but to complete the condemnation of sin and Satan's hordes, and to celebrate His coronation over all the universe.

BEYOND THE STORY
To Help You Think, Pray, Share and Do

1. Most people often forget the unseen realm and reality of angels and demons. What are your thoughts about angels and demons as part of human reality?

2. As you consider the suffering Jesus bore for our sins, the separation He endured from the Father and Spirit and then the added satanic oppression, how does that make you appreciate what He did for us?

3. Have you ever had to hold yourself back from getting involved when someone you loved was undergoing suffering or persecution? As you read about heaven's armies being held back from intervening while Jesus completed His mission on the cross, describe what that means to you.

4. What Jesus did on the cross was not only to pay the penalty for sin so we could be forgiven; He also won victory over Satan and all the forces of darkness. His victory on the cross gives us spiritual authority! How does that truth affect the way you think about salvation and how you live your Christian life?

WORDS FROM
THE CROSS

1

"Forgive Them"

"Father, forgive them; for they know not what they do."
Luke 23:34, *KJV*

The words were so unexpected that stunned, puzzled faces suddenly snapped up to stare at the one who said them.

The *content* of the words, *"Father, forgive them, for they know not what they do,"* sent shock rippling across the mass of people who watched the executions.

But it was the *context* of the words that made them so incredible . . . considering *who* said those words, and who He said them *to*, and the people He said them *for* . . . considering *where* they were said, and in the context of *what* had been happening over the past hours— considering all those factors made the words more than unexpected; they were nearly unbelievable.

A supernatural timeline had shifted into high gear only a mere 12 hours before as the deepening dusk and lengthening evening shadows across Jerusalem signaled the beginning of the annual Passover meal in every Jewish home.

It was in the flickering candlelight of one particular Passover meal in an upper room that the final countdown to the day that forever changed history began, stimulating a series of staggering events that are etched on humanity's memory and identity:

Tender words spoken by the sovereign Savior who first took a servant's towel to wash His disciple's feet . . .

A sudden turn in the time-honored tradition of the Passover meal that signaled an eternal shift in how we view salvation—now to be found in the sacrifice of one Man instead of countless Passover lambs . . .

Treason and betrayal bought at the price of a slave—30 pieces of silver—and yet one last redemptive invitation to Judas as Jesus shared the last piece of the Passover meal with him . . .

A traitor walking out into the darkness of the night . . . the darkness of chosen sin . . .

Tears and groans in a garden as the Son wrestled with the coming price He would pay for others' sin . . .

Trusting surrender to the Father's will . . .

Tired disciples asleep when it mattered most . . .

A troublesome throng armed to the teeth to arrest the most peaceful Man that ever lived . . .

Treacherous betrayal sealed with a searing kiss . . .

A trial by night that broke almost every law in the book, turning justice right side down . . .

The ringing testimony of Jesus confirming His deity as He answered the question, "Are you the Messiah, the Son of God?" with the words "I AM!"

Tyrants, garbed in robes of spiritual leadership, trampling truth for the sake of political and financial power . . .

Thugs masquerading as religious leaders battering His face into a bloody, bruised, disfigured, nearly unrecognizable mass of flesh . . .

Time alone down in an isolated prison pit, giving Jesus a foretaste of a grave to come . . .

A timid man named Pilate hiding behind the trappings of Roman authority, ignoring the warning in the troubled dreams of his wife, who understood far more than she realized . . .

A thrill-seeking puppet king named Herod who sought amusement instead of atonement . . .

Threats from religious leaders, and a crazed crowd whipped into a frenzy that forced the trade of a life—Jesus' for Barabbas's . . . injustice at the price of political expediency . . .

Taunts, stinging jabs, slugging blows, spiteful mockery by soldiers playing out a bizarre ritual they called "the King's Game," designed to give maximum emotional humiliation that blended with physical pain . . .

Thorns representing a crown slammed down on a lacerated, bloody head . . .

Torture beyond description from the hands of soldiers administering lashes from bone and metal shrapnel at the end of the cat-o'-nine tails. The whipping left Jesus' body shredded to the bone from ankles to neck, His blood splattering the ground and those around Him . . .

Tormented, staggering steps through the winding, narrow streets of Jerusalem, through an even narrower maze of shouting, pushing, weeping, howling, wildly gesturing, demonically energized people until He could no longer carry the heavy, splintered cross designed to deliver His death . . .

Timely but unexpected help, from a startled pilgrim named Simon of Cyrene, to carry the cross out the city gate and up the rocky slope to a stony summit called Golgotha that bore an eerie resemblance to a human skull . . .

Time—it was now the time for Jesus to accomplish the purpose for which He had been born.

Time to die.

At last they were at the place of crucifixion . . . three condemned men . . . two desperate to be anywhere else, one destined to be there and nowhere else, determined to follow through on what He had come there to do.

For the soldiers, the grim business of crucifixion was a common but ugly part of their job description. They had used crucifixion to put to death more than 30,000 people in the troublesome province of Palestine. Crucifixion as a means of capital punishment had been borrowed by the Persians or Phoenicians, depending on who you listened to, but the Romans had perfected it as the most excruciating, humiliating, elongated form of execution known to man.

The process was designed to bring the condemned man to the very edge of death, emotionally as well as physically, even before the final nails were driven in. Stripped naked, beaten relentlessly, mocked incessantly, paraded inexorably in the most public way as a threatening reminder to all who watched, the prisoner was laid bare to the core of his body, soul and spirit and brought to the end of every resource he had. Yet crucifixion was intended to stretch the agony even further.

The soldiers approached this crucifixion of three more convicts with a sense of bored familiarity. What they did not realize was that the crucifixion of the man on the middle cross would be unlike any other they'd ever done—they would never forget the death of this one man. Carrying the cross, the instrument of His death, Jesus finally arrived at the place that marked the end of His crucifixion journey. They tore off His clothes, dividing a pair of sandals, a headpiece, a belt, and a robe-like garment among them. Not wanting to ruin His seamless robe, they decided to gamble for it later.

A cloth was wound around Jesus' waist and hips and between His thighs with the loose end tucked in at the back. Thrown down on the rough, splintered upright piece, soldiers grabbed each arm and stretched them across the crosspiece, kneeling on the prisoner's biceps to pin Him down and place His palms upward. The executioner knelt, grabbing several rusty six-inch square spikes still blood-stained from previous uses and placed the tip at a hollow place on the wrist where two bones left a gap. Ironically, that place was just past where the so-called lifeline on the palm ended. A muscular arm raised a metal mallet and brought it down with a ringing blow, driving the nail between the two bones and through a knot of nerve and muscle once, then twice to make sure the condemned man could not struggle free.

The sharp sound of metal on metal driven through flesh into the wood brought the howling mob to shocked silence; only scattered muffled gasps and whimpering across the multitude could be heard.

It is a gruesome thing to hear nails being driven through human flesh.

Then they bent Jesus' knees and placed His feet one on top of the other, right foot over left. Sharp, ringing blows signaled another nail driven through the top of each foot and into the wooden cross, attaching the one fated for death to His final place of suffering suspended between earth and sky . . . between heaven and hell.

The executioner stepped away, and the four soldiers assigned to the cross hoisted it up by the crosspiece, dragging it until it fell with a dull thud into a hole in the ground; and with that thud the roaring of the crowd began again, especially when they saw the sign Pilate had stubbornly directed the soldiers to nail above Jesus' head. It read "Jesus of Nazareth, King of the Jews." That insightful inscription incited even more infuriated invectives from the mob.

The *act* of crucifixion was swift and stunning—*dying* by crucifixion was designed for maximum pain and suffering that stretched out over hours or even days. The Romans wanted to inflict the utmost

anguish on the prisoner without allowing him to lapse into uncon-
sciousness. Crucifixion did that to the most horrific degree.

To those who watched, death appeared to come from accumulated fatigue and blood loss. The four wounds themselves were not
supposed to be fatal; their placement were instead designed to inflict the most agony possible. The nails driven into the wrists would
shatter carpal tunnel bones and tear carpal ligaments, but would
also rupture the sensorimotor median nerve, causing spasms of searing pain up and down each arm and into the shoulders and upper
back. The victim of crucifixion would suffer constant waves of nau-
sea, fever, intense thirst, cramps and spasms of intense pain all over
his body.

Death was a combination of several factors; but the worst was
slow, relentless suffocation. The crucified man would hang down,
arms in a V, suspended by the nails through his wrists. Hanging thus
by the arms, the pectoral muscles were paralyzed and the intercostal
muscles of the chest unable to act. Air could be drawn into the lungs
but not exhaled. To do that, Jesus had to push up on the spike driven
through His feet, sending off another wave of searing pain as all His
weight was on the spike. It allowed Him to bring His head up far
enough to exhale. Then the pain in His feet would be so great and the
cramps in His legs so severe that He'd have to slump back down, suspended again by His wrists until forced to push Himself up again to
breathe. The agonizing cycle continued breath by tortured breath for
hours. It was incalculable pain—cycles of searing spasms and cramps;
raw burning, throbbing flesh as the shredded back rubbed up and
down, again and again, on the splintered wood. Partial asphyxiation
progressively became permanent suffocation.

Then another stage of the agony would begin. Deep, crushing
weight pressed on the chest as the pericardium slowly filled with
serum and began to crush the heart. Deprived of liquid and oxygen,
the blood thickened. The heart struggled to pump the heavy, thick
blood even as it was being crushed by lungs filling with fluid—a syrup
of water mixed with blood.

Physical death mercifully arrived with the combination of dehydration, asphyxiation, congestive heart failure, shock and blood loss.
This was the physical death Jesus submitted Himself to.

Heaped upon the unbearable physical pain was the emotional humiliation—the continual jeering, taunts, spiteful words and curses hurled at Jesus . . . verbal vomit heaved on Him as He hung there by soldiers, Scribes, Sadducees, Pharisees and countless others across the crowd who were caught up in the mass hysteria—all infected and infused with demonic support from the realm of the spirit.

It was in that context that Jesus spoke those nearly unbelievable words. The original language suggests that He spoke them more than once as He endured crucifixion.

"Father, forgive them . . . they know not what they do."

It was those words that made heads snap up in shock, straining to comprehend what He was saying, realizing in stunned amazement that He was *praying* . . . for *them*.

The words of His prayer were unlike any the crowd around the cross had ever heard before.

Jesus called God "Father." To the hardened Roman soldiers whose allegiance was pledged to Caesar, the idea of any god being called "father" was beyond their realm of spiritual understanding. Their views of God were many, because they had many gods, each with a particular realm of power and set of expectations. There was a god for every conceivable area of life. The gods were fickle and selfish, demanding heavy sacrifices around elaborate rituals in order to be appeased. On a whim, a god could punish or prosper someone, regardless of the payment and worship given to them. There was even a god of revenge, which they called on often to punish their enemies. Above all the unseen gods was Caesar, the human manifestation of the power and might of Rome. To a Roman, a god was to be feared, appeased and approached only through elaborate rituals and pleading. Any concept of god as "father" did not fit into Roman thinking.

The Jews around the cross, from religious leaders to apathetic, occasional Temple attendees, were also stunned to hear Jesus call God "Father." Although the Word of God revealed many names for God, most people saw Him as distant, unapproachable and unknowable except at certain times, in certain places, represented by certain religious leaders, through certain rituals and the blood of countless animal sacrifices. Whether called Creator, King, Lord, Judge—even saying the name of God was restricted by their religion. To call God "Father" was too close, too intimate, too personal—out of the reach of regular people and even out of reach to religious professionals.

Yet Jesus called God "Father," revealing the true nature of a God of love, provision, protection, mercy, strength, holiness, justice, grace, forgiveness, generosity . . . a God who gives life instead of taking it.

Not only did Jesus call God "Father," but He also prayed, *"forgive them . . ."*

Forgive?! The soldiers had heard prayers of desperation many times, prayers that pleaded innocence or blamed someone else—anyone else—instead of taking personal responsibility for choices and actions; prayers that cursed the soldiers; prayers for release from the pain; prayers to be delivered from punishment; prayers for escape from the situation; prayers that either irritated the soldiers or that they intentionally ignored.

But never before had they ever heard a prayer asking forgiveness for *them* . . . and the realization shocked them, especially the Centurion. Before the awful day was done, the Centurion would confess that the man on the middle cross was truly the Son of God.

The Jewish religious leaders were also stunned; they had mockingly invited Jesus to come down off the cross and save Himself to prove that He was the Messiah. Now they realized that He was staying on the cross to save *them* . . . and to the memory of more than one scriptural scribe came the words of Isaiah 53:12, written seven centuries before:

He poured out his life unto death,
    and was numbered with the transgressors.
    For he bore the sin of many,
        and made intercession for the transgressors.

In the face of the most monstrous injustice in history, the sinless Son of God asked for the forgiveness of those who sinned against Him that day, and for all who would sin against Him on every subsequent day of history.

Before that awful day was done, one of the criminals crucified next to Jesus would receive the answer to Jesus' prayer for his forgiveness and his own request for pardon. Forgiveness is our greatest need and God's greatest gift.

" . . . for they know not what they do . . ."

The closing words of Christ's simple prayer made His intercession even more incredible. He was pleading their case for them! Ignorance does not invalidate responsibility for sin, but Jesus was intensely aware of what those around Him at the cross "knew not" that day.

They *"knew not"* the nature of God who loved them so much that He was giving the life of His only Son so that those who would put their faith in Him would not perish but have eternal life. God did not send His Son to condemn the world but to save the world . . .

They *"knew not"* the desperate need of their hearts, deceived by selfishness, depraved by the deceitfulness of sin. They knew not the distance their sins had separated them from God.

They *"knew not"* the necessity of the sacrifice of the sinless Son of God as the only possible substitute that could satisfy the justice of a holy God.

They *"knew not"* the nearness of the saving forgiveness Jesus would give them if they would only come to Him in simple, repentant, humble faith.

They *"knew not"* . . . so they did what they did thinking they were in the right when they could not have been more wrong.

Yet, that incredible, nearly unbelievable prayer for forgiveness that Jesus uttered on the cross opened the door that day and every day afterward for those who would come to believing faith. His excruciating death opened the door for us to experience eternal life. His request to the Father still opens the door for our redemption and a true, personal, intimate, life-giving relationship with God as our Father . . . because He prayed, "Father, forgive them for they know not what they do" on *that* day, we now can pray *this* day, "Father, forgive *me,* for I know what I have done . . . Father, *forgive* me, for I know what Jesus has done for me."

Have you ever prayed that prayer in humble faith? Have you ever personally experienced the forgiveness that Jesus purchased for us on the cross? You can experience it if you'll come to Him today. His sacrificial death makes possible our spiritual birth.

And because of what Jesus prayed on the cross that day, *today* the Father will answer your prayer for forgiveness and open the door that leads to a relationship with Him that lasts forever. Because Jesus has shut down sin, death and hell, the door to heaven is now open through Him.

Jesus' prayer *that* Good Friday allows us to pray *this* Good Friday—
or any other day—to a Father who forgives.

BEYOND THE STORY
To Help You Think, Pray, Share and Do

1. Most depictions of Jesus' death on Calvary acknowledge crucifixion, but rarely do we "see" the full horror of it. As death by crucifixion was described, how did that affect the way you now understand what Jesus was willing to do for you?

2. Few religions have a picture of God as "Father" or the possibility of being in a loving, redemptive, intimate family relationship with Him. How does Jesus' praying to God as "Father" affect the way you view God and your relationship with Him?

3. "Forgive them . . ." No one has ever faced such undeserved injustice as Jesus. Yet His response was to pray for those who were unjust to be forgiven. All of us have been hurt and treated wrongfully by others. How do you pray for those who have wronged you?

4. Forgiveness is a divine decision; God forgives us with His divine love, then gives us His divine grace to be able to forgive others. Read Ephesians 4:32. What are the implications in that verse of Scripture for you? What decisions do you need to make in light of Jesus' example and empowering love?

2

"TODAY . . . PARADISE"

"I tell you the truth, today you will be with me in paradise."
LUKE 23:43, *NIV*

The drama that led to the climax of human history unfolded rapidly over the course of one day's span of time. At every point of His journey, from Gethsemane to Calvary, Jesus encountered people who were searching—some blinded by hate and searching only to destroy Him; others searching for the truth, opening their hearts for the first time.

Those opposite extremes come into sharp focus in the persons of the two ruffians who were crucified on either side of Jesus that day we now call Good Friday.

Today we meet those two men in their last moments of life as they meet Jesus mounted on His last pulpit.

The morning sun had risen high over the valley, burning off the mists of the early part of the day. It shone down over the city of Jerusalem and warmed the people who lived there. Today was going to be hot, yet no one would ever remember this day for the temperature.

Hanging suspended between heaven and earth on a hill called the Skull, three men were writhing on rough, rugged crosses, mingling their blood with the splinters of the wood against their backs.

Crucifixion was only one of the ugly ways the Romans used to execute condemned men. But it was far and away the cruelest and most frightening for people to watch, and the most excruciating and horrible for those who were condemned to die that way.

Each prisoner had carried his own crossbeam through the winding, narrow streets of Jerusalem, out the western city gate and up the hill known as Golgotha—the place of the skull.

At the top of the hill, which overlooked the city dump and constantly had the stench of burning refuse wafting over its crest, the men had been forced onto their backs (which had already been shredded by the flesh-tearing lashes of the cat-o'-nine-tails) and onto the main beam of each cross. Their arms were then stretched out along the crosspiece and nailed to the wood with rusty, often used, metal spikes. After much practice, the Romans had found two small bones in the wrist that could hold the weight of a human body without the hands tearing away from the nails. The rest of the body could "rest" on a wooden stirrup-like saddle, the feet nailed together with another spike at the bottom of the cross.

Death on the cross was almost never from bleeding. Rather, infection from the dirty nails began immediately and was hurried along by the already weakened condition of the man fastened to the wood by them. But the main cause of death on a cross almost always came from asphyxiation. Each breath was gained by forcing the body up off the foot saddle, and gasping as one does when coming to the top of water while swimming, one breath was gained until the process needed to be repeated. Slowly, surely, the weight of the person's body robbed him of the precious air he needed to live.

Death came slowly in many cases. It was not uncommon for prisoners to be on the cross for a week. For others, mercifully, it came sooner.

Such was the status of the three men on the crosses this day.

The middle cross bore the person of "Jesus of Nazareth, King of the Jews," as proclaimed by the sign Pilate had put above His head. The man on the right, tradition tells us, was named Dysmas; on the left cross was Gestus. Both were convicted criminals, perhaps linked to the man Jesus was substituted for that day—Barabbas.

Below them was a great crowd of people, some taunting, some crying in heart-breaking sorrow, some in mute shock. Unseen but present were the forces of heaven and hell as well. Strangely enough, the cries and curses were all directed to the middle cross, and that fact did not escape the notice of the two men on either side of Jesus.

They had noticed when Jesus had refused the cheap drugged wine of grape juice, given in order to deaden the pain. They themselves had readily drunk, hoping to escape some of the agony of the physical judgment of the cross.

They noticed His reaction to the men who had nailed Him down. He had not cursed at them, nor swore revenge against them. They had heard His first words spoken from the cross as He looked down at the soldiers and the people:

"Father, forgive them, for they do not know what they are doing."

Why, that had sounded like a plea for mercy for them, rather than a curse of condemnation!

Two hours passed. Minutes were marked by blood drops under the crosses. The pain became increasingly agonizing; the shouts and taunts of the crowd and the mockery of the soldiers beat on them like a mallet pounding on the stretched skin of a drum. Jesus' head moved uneasily against the cross as a sick man does against a hot pillow. He carried on Him not only the weight of His own body, but also the entire weight of the sin of all humanity . . . for all time.

Suddenly the sky grew dark, but no stars were visible in the blackened sky. It was high noon, but it resembled a moonless midnight. A chill swept over the vast crowd, partially from the sharp temperature drop and partially from the eerie sense that the sun and stars themselves refused to look on the travesty they were illuminating. Their Creator was being killed by those He had made and come to redeem, and it was as if they could not bear to watch.

The attention of the two men on either side of Jesus was even more acutely focused on Him now. Nothing had ever happened like this at any other public execution. They were aware more than ever that the man on the middle cross was more than just a man.

Suddenly, Gestus spoke from the cross on Jesus' left. His words, each one spat out with effort, came out in an angry, pain-crazed stream: "Aren't you the Christ? Save yourself . . . and us!" Then a spasm of pain wracked his body and he began to curse and swear, blaming Jesus for his pain.

The words of Gestus are like the reaction of so many who face the cross of consequences for their own sins:

"I'm not responsible for my sins."

"I want deliverance from my consequences, not my condemnation."

"Deliver me from my pain, not my punishment."

"How could God do this to me?"

This thief wanted salvation from a cross and nails and pain, not from his sin and the hell his own deeds had brought him.

To Gestus, Jesus made no reply, for the Lord does not respond to prayers like that.

Now a voice came from Jesus' right hand, from Dysmas, and rebuked Gestus.

"Don't you even fear God when you are dying? We deserve to die for our evil deeds, but this man hasn't done one thing wrong."

Then, turning to Jesus, his face desperate through the pain, his heart pleading, he said, "Jesus, remember me when You come into Your Kingdom." In effect he was saying, "Put in a good word for me, will You?"

In those words Dysmas spoke the heart of every repentant person coming to the cross:

"I deserve to die for my sins."

"I'm on the edge of eternity . . . my choice decides my fate."

"Jesus Christ is my only hope."

"Lord, I've sinned; please forgive me."

Jesus lifted His head and turned to Dysmas. Even in the midst of the great pain He was suffering, He still had time to hear the prayer of a needy, humble heart. For the first time since He had been raised on the cross, He smiled, and the sparkle returned to His eyes. Speaking in a clear, strong voice, He spoke the words Dysmas longed to hear:

"I tell you the truth, this very day you will be with Me in Paradise. I'll do more than put in a good word for you, I'll take you with Me."

All of earth's pleading had been in the words of Dysmas. All of heaven's pardon was in Jesus' response.

For Gestus, the reply had fallen on unhearing ears and a hardened heart. He had the same opportunity as Dysmas but had rejected Jesus' offer of eternal life . . . forever.

Those powerful words Jesus spoke to a dying criminal are life words to the dying race of humanity, and in them we find hope, invitation and the opportunity to receive His forgiveness:

"Its never too late to be forgiven."

"No matter what your past, the cross pays the price for sin."

"Salvation is ours not by how we feel, but on Jesus' promise."

"Death is the immediate doorway into eternity."

"Jesus is waiting and willing to forgive those who come to Him in humble repentance."

The dying man, comforted—and for the first time in his life, living with hope—smiled back at Jesus and set his lips to endure to the end.

"Today you will be with me in Paradise" . . . life words spoken to a ruffian who came to Him in repentance. You see, we all deserve to be on one of those crosses next to Jesus, because sin has always carried the sentence of death; yet we have a choice of how we will respond to the Man on the middle cross, as did the ruffians. We can choose as Gestus did—we can reject Jesus' forgiveness, or we can choose as Dysmas did—we can repent and receive eternal life.

When we think about that ruffian who met Christ while he was at his crossing point into eternity, it should make us smile because we know we also don't deserve love like that. None of us do. When you get right down to it, any contribution any of us make is pretty puny. All of us—even the best of us—deserve heaven about as much as that crook did. All of us are signing on Jesus' credit account, not our own.

It also should make us smile in wonder that there is a grinning ex-con, walking streets of gold, who knows more about grace firsthand than the theorizing of a thousand theologians. Firsthand experience always trumps abstract education.

In the crowd that day, no one else would have given an expiring thief a chance. He didn't appear to have a prayer. Yet, he did pray . . . simply trusting the One next to him as the only hope he had. In the end, that's all he had. And in the end, that's all he needed. It was his ticket to Paradise.

It's ours too.

BEYOND THE STORY
To Help You Think, Pray, Share and Do

1. It's been said that crisis doesn't make character, it reveals it. The suffering the two thieves experienced on the cross revealed who they really were on the inside. What have your times of suffering revealed about you?

2. Some people only see their circumstances through the limited lens of their finite understanding of fairness. Unwilling to accept responsibility for the consequences of their actions, people often blame God instead. Have you ever blamed God for difficult times? What does this story teach you?

3. Salvation is available right up to the moment of death. With our last breath we can pray for God's forgiveness and receive it. If you've been praying for someone a long time and they've not made a move toward Christ yet, take heart. Keep praying. Keep trusting that God's persistent love is reaching out to them. Never give up on them; Jesus hasn't.

4. Death is the doorway to eternity. Take a moment to imagine what happened to the thief that Jesus took with Him to Paradise . . . imagine him as he walked through that doorway to heaven. For all of those who know Jesus as Savior, that will someday be their experience as well! Praise God for that hope.

3

"WHY?"

"My God, my God, why have you forsaken me?"
MATTHEW 27:46, *NIV*

Even though He knew it was coming, it was still nearly too much to bear.

Before the Godhead had laid down the foundations of creation, they had laid out the plan of redemption. Father, Son and Spirit, looking down on "time" from beginning to end, because they stood outside and above it, had looked ahead to this day with expectation and deliberation. Of all the days that would be identified by the rising and setting of the sun they had created, this day would stand out from all the rest. Together they would accomplish their mission of redeeming creation in a way that was unfathomable from a human perspective and only possible through the power of the diety . . . the Son would be forsaken as He bore sin, yet the unity of the Trinity would remain unbroken . . . and they would do it because of love.

They had coexisted in a perpetual dance of delight, intimacy, holy love and creativity—three Persons of one infinite essence, one eternal Godhead of three individuals, complete and perfect in themselves. Yet, they had chosen to express their creativity and generosity by speaking creation into existence so they could share their love, and then they shaped a man and a woman in their own image.

Amongst all the shimmering, iridescent angelic beings; amongst the nearly unlimited brilliant display of stars, planets and other stunning substances comprising multitudes of glowing galaxies; amongst all the glories of mountains, oceans, valleys and the lavish beauties of flora and fauna; amongst all the minutely intricate to immense members of animals who swam, flew, crawled and covered ground on paws and hooves; amongst all the splendors of Truine creative genius, the man and the woman were the apex of all creation, the highest and closest to the Three-in-One, for they bore Their image and could choose to love like They did.

And then the woman and the man chose not to.

The choice to exert their own will in defiance of the Lord God's creation criteria forever changed the relationship of God with humanity; it also contaminated creation itself. Sin separated, contaminated and began to disintegrate creation on every level. The man and the woman were infected with self-interest, altering how they would relate to the Lord and to each other. The perfection of the Creator's plan had been corrupted by human volition, and to repair it would require Divine intervention. Creator would now have to also become Redeemer.

The Godhead had known this would happen, and even with their foreknowledge they had chosen to share their love, even with the risk that it would be rejected. Father, Son and Spirit had mapped out a plan so amazing in its implications that even the angels longed to fully understand it. The Trinity, who stood above all creation and outside of time, would willingly enter the world of humanity as one of them. The Son of God would put on a robe of human flesh and become the Son of Man—fully God, fully man—and He alone would be able to repair the vast breach of sinful severance and bring a holy God back into relationship with fallen men and women. He would be born of a woman, grow up in an ordinary Jewish home with a Messianic family tree and experience the joys and tears of the human condition. He would identify with those He came to save in every way except choosing to sin as every other human had. And then He would bridge the great divide and reunite creation to Creator by giving Himself as the sacrifice that would address the sin problem, bringing redemption, reconciliation, restoration and relationship between God and humanity once again.

The Trinity didn't keep the plan a secret. From the very earliest days in the Garden they began to promise the fallen ones that fellowship was possible again. Over the course of generations the promises continued, and godly prophets hand-selected by God began to paint a picture of the plan. The plan included physical, temporal representations through a Temple that illustrated the holiness of God, sacred gatherings throughout the year to remind people of God's care for them in the natural and spiritual realms, human priests to symbolize His reconciliation, a sacrificial system where spotless animals spilled blood to cover sin—all of which had to be repeated continually because they were all imperfect representations. The picture included wonderfully bright brushstrokes of hope—portraying the pardon, deliverance, restoration, forgiveness and reign of the Son when He would arrive.

The picture also included somber hues of the price that the Son would have to pay—accusation, rejection, subjection to horrific abuse . . . crucifixion. Redemption would include bearing all the accumulated actions and consequences of every man and woman who had ever lived and would ever live. It would also include the ultimate price for the Son—being forsaken by His Father, who could not allow sin in His presence. The Son who knew no sin would become sin on behalf of humanity, and in so doing, He would feel deserted by Father and Spirit. That separation would be hardest of all.

The plan unfolded according to their Sovereign will and brought the Son at last to a skull-shaped hill and death on a wooden cross.

He'd been hanging between heaven and earth for nearly six hours. The last three had been in total darkness that began at high noon. Creation itself could not bear to watch what was being done to the Creator, and the sun had refused to shine. It was as if a curtain was being closed to block out all light—a darkness that was literal and supernatural.

The Son had endured physical and emotional punishment from human and demonic sources beyond what any human had ever endured before. Through it all the companionship of the Three had been unbroken, and that fellowship sustained the Son in the midst of this horrific situation. It was as if a supernatural shaft of light connected heaven and Son, infusing Him with the strength He needed to endure.

He'd spoken little over the six hours He'd been on the cross— He prayed that the Father would forgive the ones who had condemned and crucified Him; He promised pardon and Paradise to the repentant thief to His right; and He provided care for His beloved mother. It was extremely difficult to breathe, much less talk, so every word came with great exertion.

In the Temple, the Passover lamb was being carried to the altar where it would figuratively bear the weight of the nation's sins for an entire year. As that lamb was being brought to the altar of sacrifice, something shifted in the spiritual realm. Suddenly the Son looked up, His eyes wide as He saw a reality unseen by others and that only He could understand. A door in heaven was closing, cutting off the shaft of light that represented the connection of the Three. At the same time, an incalculable weight of iniquity was rolled on His broad, bloodied shoulders, invading His very being. It covered Him, smothered Him, crushed Him, shut Him off from the light from above. The door above closed. The Light was gone.

He felt alone. Completely and infinitely alone.

A holy God had separated Himself from sin, even though it was being borne by a sinless Son.

Jesus gasped at the magnitude of the malignant mass He now bore . . . individual sins coursing from the very source of sin itself . . . *attitudes* like arrogance, envy, jealousy, rage, malice, lust, pride, greed, thirst for power; *actions* like theft, lying, adultery, sodomy, abuse, addiction, control, exploitation—all flowing from the central core of selfishness that rebelled against the rightful rule of God.

All the consequences of those sins imploded on Him, the rippling effects across nations, generations, centuries, families, now reversing themselves to heap solely on Him.

Grief, despair, fear, depression, terror, rage, insecurity, anxiety, paranoia, hopelessness . . .

In His body, He bore the very effects of the curse of sin in its physical dimensions—cancer, blindness, deafness, leprosy, malaria, plague, polio, genetic deformities . . . suffering in all its forms piled on top of the excruciating pain He was already enduring.

All of hell's fury pummeled Him with its hatred of holiness.

And on top of it all came the reality of being severed from the very presence of a God of holy love. He knew it was coming, but it was far worse than He could have humanly imagined. He'd never known His Father's wrath; now He was drinking to the dregs the cup of sin in all its hellish horror and consequences, draining it to the last drop.

A groan of desperation rose from the depths of His being, rising from a heart broken, deserted and disowned, His face looking upward into the darkness, tears running down shredded cheeks, a lone voice crying out, calling home . . .

"*Eloi, Eloi! Lama sabachthani?*"

"My God . . . my God! *Why* have *You* forsaken Me?"

There was no answer; He knew there wouldn't be. There couldn't be. That was the plan.

Below Him, faces looked up, some puzzled, some amused, others astonished. The Roman soldiers were bewildered. They'd heard dying men bargaining with deity for mercy, but this was different somehow. They knew from their own experience what it was like to call on a god in times of trouble—a god they hadn't given the time of day to before the crisis. But this man sounded like He was crying out to family.

Some of the religious leaders who had been jeering and mocking earlier until they'd grown hoarse and the darkness had reduced them to uneasy murmurs, now gloated. "He's calling for Elijah . . . this pretend prophet wants another prophet to rescue him!" Others joined in. "Yes . . . let's see if Elijah comes to save him. Nobody else is!" They all knew the popular belief that Elijah would rescue those in deep trouble. Every Jewish family left an empty place setting at their Passover meals in hopes that Elijah would come, announcing the coming of the Messiah and His Kingdom. Cackling laughter punctuated insult with irony, not realizing that the man on the middle cross was staying there to save *them*.

But others among the priests and elders were astounded. They knew those words. Jesus was quoting Scripture. He was quoting scriptural truths they'd memorized and known since childhood that now came into stark focus in their minds, demanding their attention.

Psalm 22 was coming to life in front of them!

Without realizing that they were doing it, several of them began to repeat the words from memory in astonished realization and hushed awe:

> *My God, my God, why have you forsaken me?*
> *Why do you remain so distant?*
> *Why do you ignore my cries for help?*
> *Every day I call out to you . . . every night you hear my voice, but*
> *I find no relief. . . .*

*I am a worm and not a man. I am scorned and despised by all!
Everyone who sees me mocks me. They sneer and shake their heads,
saying, "Is this the one who relies on the LORD? Then let the LORD save
him! If the LORD loves him so much, let the LORD rescue him!"*

*Do not stay so far from me, for trouble is near, and no one else
can help me.*

*My enemies surround me like a herd of bulls; fierce bulls of
Bashan have hemmed me in!*

*Like roaring lions attacking their prey, they come at me with gap-
ing mouths.*

*My life is poured out like water,
And all my bones are out of joint.
My heart is like wax, melting within me.
My strength has dried up like sunbaked clay.
My tongue sticks to the roof of my mouth.
You have laid me in the dust and left me for dead.
My enemies surround me like a pack of dogs,
An evil gang closes in on me.
They have pierced my hands and feet.
I can count every bone in my body.
My enemies stare at me and gloat.
They divide my clothes among themselves and throw dice for my
garments . . .*

It was all happening. Here! Now! Before their very eyes the picture of the Messiah was being revealed to them, the salvation plan of
the Sovereign One on display for all who had eyes to see. Some of them
trembled in dawning realization.

The divine justice of God now took action against sin—punishing,
rescuing, cleansing, delivering, restoring, purifying . . .

. . . and then the load was gone, erased by grace, lifted by love, paid
for by the only One who could make the transaction.

To the physical eye, the darkness remained. But in the unseen
realm a door flung open and light streamed down.

Fellowship restored . . .

Forgiveness purchased . . .

The Three as One completing Their mission of redemption.

He was almost done. Just a few moments to go. He headed toward the conclusion the Godhead had designed.

He who had been forsaken for our sakes . . .

He who had paid a price we could not pay had now made fellowship with God possible for fallen ones, once again.

All just as They planned.

BEYOND THE STORY
To Help You Think, Pray, Share and Do

1. God's always up to something bigger than we realize. Many times our current situation doesn't make sense or doesn't appear to be fair; but later we see that God had a bigger plan in mind. What's going on in your life right now that you need to trust God for because He's up to something bigger than you can recognize right now?

2. Have you ever felt forsaken by those you needed most? How did you respond?

3. Do you know someone who might be feeling very alone right now? How can you come alongside to minister to them in their time of need?

4. Hebrew 13:5 promises us, "Never will I leave you; never will I forsake you." Claim that promise for yourself and others who need the comfort and hope of that promise.

4

"BEHOLD YOUR SON"

"Woman, behold your son!"
JOHN 19:26, *NKJV*

"And a sword will pierce your own soul too."

For a moment she was 16 again, holding her week-old Son in her arms and listening to an old man's prophetic message, his gnarled hand gently resting on her head. He spoke of an event in the future, yet the compassionate pain in his eyes as he looked at her was if he were seeing it firsthand. Her eyes large under the protective hand of the prophet Simeon, all she could do was hold her baby closer to her heart and nod in partial understanding. But those words continued to echo in her heart long afterward.

That had been thirty-three years ago. Now the words were coming to life before her tear-blurred eyes. Just above her, her Son was suspended on the coarse, splintered wood of a cross, struggling in agony for each breath. Around her swirled a sickening vortex of sights, smells and sounds—the stench of burning garbage wafting over the hill from the hellish pit below; the strident shouts of people badgering and blaspheming her Son; the stony apathy of the Roman soldiers watching three men die; the surging crowd behind her; the smug approval of the religious leaders; the sudden, eerie darkness that had descended three hours into the awful crucifixion process; the sobs of her own sister and the other women with her at the foot of the cross; the strong arms of her nephew John around her and his mother. But she had eyes and ears and heart only for her Son, hanging on a cross with spikes protruding from his wrists and feet.

Her Son . . . had it been so long ago? It seemed like only yesterday that her husband, Joseph, and her Son Jesus were handling nails like those in their carpenter's shop as father and son labored over another project. From the time He slept in the wooden cradle His father had made, Jesus had always loved being around the wood and stone tools of a master craftsman. He learned the trade from Joseph, patiently practicing the skills day by day until He at last could shape and fashion wood and stone into useful and beautiful objects. How she loved watching the two laughing together as sunlight splashed on their workbench, calloused carpenters' hands in perfect harmony as they labored together.

She had loved watching their son grow up. Miraculously conceived, His birth announcement sung by the angelic choir of heaven itself, she had always known her Son was unique among all the people who walked or would ever walk the face of the earth. Yet, so much of those growing years had been so . . . ordinary. Many days, she caught herself watching Him, musing to herself that the Messiah was eating her soup for lunch . . . the Son of God was thanking *her* for His daily bread.

There were times that reminded her that He was here on a mission that reached far beyond their small business in Nazareth. That time when he was 12 . . . they thought they'd lost Him on the way home from a trip to Jerusalem. After days of frantic searching, they had found Him in the Temple, matching wits and discussing mature theology with the professors there. He had looked at them so innocently as He responded to their worried scolding. He hadn't meant to alarm them, but didn't they know He'd be in His Father's house going about His business?

There had been times when He would get a faraway look in His eyes, as if seeing far more than the natural eye could see, and farther ahead than the natural mind could envision. His grandparents, aunts and uncles commented often about what an unusually mature boy He was for His age as they watched Him play with His brothers, sisters and cousins.

It was when she heard Him pray that Mary could most see what only she and Joseph knew . . . the easy familiarity in which He addressed His heavenly Father, the joy He took in worship, the way He could see His heavenly Father's hand in all things . . . those were the times when she knew her Son would not stay in Nazareth forever. His mission was much larger.

He'd stayed in Nazareth after Joseph died, caring for her and the rest of the family; running the business; mentoring His brothers in carpentry skills; being a blessing to their entire community. Everyone expected Him to carry on the heritage of another generation of craftsmen as His father and grandfather before Him. Inside, however, Mary knew it was only temporary.

One day He'd walked into the house as the lengthening shadows and red glow on the horizon were marking the end of another day. He'd looked at her, not saying anything, but in His eyes she could see that His larger journey had begun. Still not completely understanding, she'd given her blessing. He'd made sure she was cared for, turning over the business to His brothers with everything in perfect order. That was just like Him.

For three years He traveled, taught and transformed people all over their land. Stories got back to her—some wondrous, some preposterous—about what He was doing. From time to time He'd stop at home to see her—always too short a visit—and He'd pick her up in His strong arms and hug her to His heart, kissing her cheek softly as He left again. So many times she'd wanted to ask Him to stay, but she knew He was a Man on a mission, and she'd let Him go, always promising her love and prayers. His grateful smile and the look in His eyes as He left warmed her heart for days after.

Their whole extended family normally came to the Passover feast in Jerusalem each year, but this year she instinctively knew that it was vital for her to be there. She needed to be near Him, because in her heart she knew His mission was almost done.

It had been an awful week. After an entry reminiscent of a king coming in peace, rumors and insinuations about Him buzzed throughout the city swollen to many times its normal size with pilgrims there for the feast. There had been the intense confrontation with the Pharisees in the Temple one day and then the sudden downward slide of events in one night that included a mockery of a trial before the Sanhedrin, an atrocious audience with Herod, a puzzling performance by Pilate, the shocking scourging by the soldiers, the blood-stained steps through the winding streets out the city gate and the final ascent to the skull-shaped hill known as Golgotha, all the while being pelted with the deafening shouts of the crowd.

She had followed the crowd with her sisters and friends, letting John push through a place for them until they stood at the foot of the cross. It was all she could do to lift her eyes to the horrific sight in front of her; but it was at the ringing blows of hammer on nails being pounded through flesh that her heart felt a stab of pain unlike anything she'd ever experienced. It was then that Simeon's words came back to her:

"... *and a sword will pierce your own soul too.*"

Now she understood. It had all come to this. But then, it had always been about this. Somewhere, somehow in her mother's heart, she'd always known. This was His mission.

She'd been looking at Him, longing to hold Him close to her heart again, watching Him forgive the very people who'd done this to Him ... and then He was looking at her.

If He hadn't been her Son, she would not have recognized Him. His face was swollen from repeated blows, soiled from sweat and spit and dirt. His beard had been yanked out in chunks, leaving the appearance of His face deformed and bleeding. Blood ran down from the rudely fashioned crown of thorns they'd smashed down on His head. Yet, when He looked at her with those gentle, loving eyes , the look of love she'd seen from them for over 30 years was unmistakable.

He winced as He pushed Himself up on the nails through His feet to gasp for a breath. Breathing was torture, speaking nearly impossible. His eyes were speaking volumes, but His words were few.

"*Woman* . . . [it was a term of respect and endearment] . . . *behold your Son.* You've raised me, loved me, sacrificed for me . . . now I am giving the ultimate sacrifice for you . . . and for all humanity." Gratitude, love, release—so much in so few words!

Then Jesus looked to John, who had his arms protectively around his mother and his aunt. *Behold . . . your mother.* He was trusting the care of His mother to the disciple who loved Him. John nodded in agreement and affirmation. To the very end, the Son was caring for His mother, making sure everything was taken care of.

Then a spasm of pain shot through Jesus' body and through her own heart and she reached out for Him, tears streaming down her face. In that vast, teeming mass of people around the cross, she understood what no one else could.

The nails He'd used on the cross now made it possible for Him to forgive and cleanse, shape and fashion the most desperate, deceitful and disfigured human heart into something redeemed, beautiful and useful. His last work with nails was the one job He'd come to do all along. The mission was now complete . . . the sacrifice made . . . the way now open for salvation offered to the entire world.

Only she could call Him Son, but from now on, the world could call Him Savior.

BEYOND THE STORY
To Help You Think, Pray, Share and Do

1. Mary had lived with a prophetic word about her Son for a long time. Many mothers seem to have an instinctive knowledge of their children's destiny. If you are a parent, especially a mother, how do you relate to that "parental discernment"? How does it affect the way you go about raising your children?

2. Mary's remarkable courage to stay close to her Son in the midst of His greatest crisis is amazing. Sometimes we don't realize we have the grace to do what seems impossible until we're in the midst of severe situations. What situation might be like that for you right now? Who needs you to "stay close in the crisis"? Take a moment and ask the Lord for the grace and courage you need to come alongside those who are most in need.

3. Take a moment and pray for your children—or grandchildren, nephews, nieces, or even children in your church. Every person has a destiny designed by God. We all have a wonderful opportunity to be a part of shaping that destiny by our influence. Ask God to fulfill His plan for them and help you play your part in His divine purposes for them.

4. Simeon's prophetic words prepared Mary for the experience at the cross. When have you had someone give you a "word from the Lord" that prepared you for something that was yet to come?

5

"I THIRST"

Jesus, knowing that all things were now accomplished, that the Scripture
might be fulfilled, said, "I thirst!"
JOHN 19:28, *NKJV*

"I thirst."
Almost done.
Prophet's words.
Prophecy fulfilled.
My reality.
"I thirst." Two words. His words. Humanity's longings. Anyone
who knew the Scriptures realized that Jesus was quoting from Psalm
69. Even to the very end, Jesus was making sure that every word of
prophecy was being fulfilled. Every word. No detail missed. What a
prophet had expressed in real despair centuries before was now being
experienced in real time by Jesus.

> *Save me, O God,*
> *   for the floodwaters are up to my neck.*
> *Deeper and deeper I sink into the mire;*
> *   I can't find a foothold to stand on.*
> *I am in deep water,*
> *   and the floods overwhelm me.*
> *I am exhausted from crying for help;*
> *   my throat is parched and dry.*
> *My eyes are swollen with weeping,*
> *   waiting for my God to help me.*
> *Those who hate me without cause*
> *   Are more numerous than the hairs on my head.*
> *   These enemies who seek to destroy me . . . attack me with lies,*
> *   demanding that I give back what I didn't steal. . . .*

For I am mocked and shamed for your sake;
  humiliation is written all over my face.
Even my own brothers pretend they don't know me;
  they treat me like a stranger.
Passion for your house burns within me,
  so those who insult you are also insulting me. . . .
But I keep right on praying to you, LORD,
  hoping this is the time you will show me favor.
  In your unfailing love, O God,
  answer my prayer with your sure salvation.
Pull me out of the mud;
  don't let me sink any deeper!
  Rescue me from those who hate me,
  and pull me from these deep waters.
Don't let the floods overwhelm me,
  or the deep waters swallow me,
  or the pit of death devour me.
Answer my prayers, O LORD,
  for your unfailing love is wonderful.
  Turn and take care of me,
  for your mercy is so plentiful.
Don't hide from your servant;
  answer me quickly, for I am in deep trouble!
Come and rescue me;
  free me from all my enemies.
You know the insults I endure—the humiliation and disgrace.
  You have seen all my enemies and know what they have said.
Their insults have broken my heart,
  and I am in despair.
  If only one person would show some pity;
  if only one would turn and comfort me.
But instead, they give me poison for food;
  they offer me sour wine for my thirst. . . .

Fully God.
  Trinity's plan.
  Father's will.

Spirit's power.
Son's submission.
Burden borne.
Darkness defeated.
Justice satisfied.
Redemption revealed.
Sin cleansed.
Sinners redeemed.
Hell overthrown.
Heaven opened.

Can God be thirsty? How is it possible that the One-in-Three who is complete in Himself could have any needs? Yet, here was Jesus, fully God, verbalizing His thirst. From God's perspective, how could He be thirsty? There's a sense of longing in those words, an expression of need from the heart of God. What was He pining for?

When He created humanity in His image, He also knew that He would be creating this kind of thirst for Himself. For the One who stands above and outside time, who looks down at history the way we look at a timeline stretching from wall to wall in children's classrooms; time, timelessness, timeliness and timing blend together beyond our understanding. The Timeless One knew there would be a time when the ones He created to enjoy His fellowship, experience His love and uniquely express His nature to the rest of creation would deliberately reject His invitation of godliness in favor of their own inferior imitation of godlikeness. At the moment of separation brought on by free will's choices—the failure of the Fall—a divine longing for reconciliation and relationship, a thirst to redeem and restore what had been lost became part of the reality of the Trinity's heart for humanity.

Fully man.
Shared suffering.
Shredded flesh.
Raging fever.
Burning throat.
Wooden tongue.
Cracked lips.

Draining blood.
Straining lungs.
Screaming muscles.
Weakening heart.
Physically fading.

Jesus, fully man, the one who knew no sin, became sin for us and bore our sickness and our pain. He experienced physical thirst in the most personal and comprehensive way of any person who has ever lived. The physical experience of crucifixion stretched His human body to the extreme limits of endurance. He experienced raging physical dehydration in the midst of slow asphyxiation; excruciating muscular contractions and expiration one drop of blood at a time. That was the experiential thirst of Jesus. Beyond that incomprehensible personal scenario was the compilation of humanity's physical thirst—every corporeal condition and medical situation from every generation. His words, "I thirst," were our description of physical weariness, woundedness and want—the dehydration of the human condition.

"I thirst."
No comfort.
Leering demons.
Jeering watchers.
Mocking soldiers.
Sarcastic words.
"Here . . . drink."
Soaked sponge.
Sour wine.
Stinging lips.
Assistance refused.

"I thirst" not only described Jesus' physical request; it also represented an emotional craving for companionship and encouragement in the dry and weary land of relational abandonment and isolation. Utterly alone in the midst of untold numbers of visible and invisible onlookers, abandoned by everyone and the One He needed most, His yearning portrays our longings for relational intimacy. We most understand our thirst for that divinely designed need for knowing and being known by someone who loves us when we don't have it. Jesus

was experiencing that relational thirst for us. He was thirsty like that so
we would not have to be.

"I thirst."
    Hyssop branch.
    Blood covers.
    Passover Lamb.
    Prophecy completed.
    Everything connected.
    Timeless plan.
    Timeline accomplished.
    Thirty-three years.
    One day.
    Six hours.
    All eternity.
    All people.
    All sin.
    Full salvation.

That thirst in the heart of God led to a divine design for another moment in time when the Fall would be reversed and everything upside
down would become right side up again—a moment when God the Son
Himself would express that eternal thirst to end sin-induced, parched
separation with grace-produced, saturated redemption. God's thirst and
ours would be met by God's supply. Only the Timeless One could step
into time like this. Only the One With No Needs could meet this need
and in so doing meet every other need the Fall had produced. Dryness on
every level, in every realm, was being drenched and saturated with victorious salvation and deliverance. The words not only represented a
prophet's personal, anguished exclamation and Jesus' literally accomplished lamentation, but our own universal aching longings—the yearn-
ings of thirsty souls everywhere expressed in those two words . . . "I thirst."

We thirst.
    Broken dreams.
    Barren spirit.
    Image marred.
    Sin-scarred.

Hopes barred.
Wounded . . . worn.
Lost . . . alone.
Lonely . . . longing.
Justice denied.
Selfish . . . straining.
Relationships ruptured.
Deceived . . . dark.
Homesick . . . heaven.

Jesus' physical thirst was in so many ways a picture of the ultimate spiritual thirst the Father created within every person made in
His image. Those around the cross could sense it more than say it.

"Bios"—mere physical life lived only in response to bodily urges
can only be satisfied for a short time. Needs satiated with pleasure of
a temporary nature soon call again, crying out for another round of
sensory stimulation and relief. "Bios"—whether purely physical or
emotional or relational becomes an unending cycle of cravings that
can never be totally filled.

In fact, "bios" is incomplete. Human lives only lived on that level
lead only to frustration. Every human heart recognizes a beckoning to
the life that only a Creator Redeemer could initiate, instill and sus-
tain. We long for life that only He can give. Life from above, like rivers
of living water flowing from our innermost beings. Not water from
an outside source poured into our mouths down parched throats for
physical relief. Living Water from above, becoming His Life from
within, flowing out to others. We need spiritual life from the inex-
haustible Source of Life.

Jesus' statement of physical thirst was understood only on the
surface level by those at the cross. Sour vinegar, stinging swollen lips,
was the soldiers' solution. Only a precious few were crying out on the
spiritual level, recognizing their real, eternal and ultimate need.

Most people settle for bios and its partial and limited passions
never completely fulfilled. Yet people strive to satisfy the needs of their
spirit in so many ways, yearning for more.

There were a few at the cross who understood the full significance
of the thirst Jesus was describing: a condemned prisoner; a Roman
centurion. In Jesus' words they recognized their own desperate need,

their thirst for Life that only Jesus could satisfy. In turning to Him, they found they would never be thirsty again for what matters most.

Even now so many settle for bios, the short-lived physical realm of existence, when they really long for Life. Short-term substitutes abound, leaving those who drink from their leaky bottles parched and pleading for something else, something more. Someone more.

"I thirst" was a description, and on a deeper level, an invitation for all those who will hear and come.

We thirst.
> He supplies.
> Mercy abounds.
> Grace inexhaustible.
> Love inexpressible.
> Peace indescribable.
> Joy incomprehensible.
> Forgiveness ready.
> Justice satisfied.
> Image restored.
> Identity secure.
> Victory won.
> Relationships reconciled.
> Hope restored.
> Holy ... whole.
> Pardoned ... pure.
> Accepted ... adopted.
> Found ... free.
> Healing released.
> Everything *Him*possible.
> Heaven waiting.
> Life eternal.

> Come ... drink.
> Drink deep.

> Welcome home.

BEYOND THE STORY
To Help You Think, Pray, Share and Do

1. When you think of Jesus as God on the cross, what stands out to you?

2. When you think of Jesus as man on the cross, what stands out to you?

3. What are you thirsty for?

4. How can you bring the "water of Life" Jesus offers to others around you? Who do you know who needs Him most today?

6

"Finished!"

When Jesus had tasted it, he said, "It is finished!"
John 19:30, *NLT*

The mission was almost completed now, the journey nearly over.
What had begun in the heart of the triune God before time was calculated was now entering its final measured minutes.

The final countdown had really started at the beginning of the
week with His entry into Jerusalem to cheering crowds tens of thousands strong. The scene now could not have been more opposite as
jeering thousands looked on.

The Triumphal Entry became a terrible execution.

Hosannas and cheers became hateful choruses of "Crucify!"

The man carried into the city on a colt left the city carrying a cross.

Palm branches waving in adoration became whip
lashes of agony.

The one lauded as conquering king now hung
on a cross as a common criminal.

None of this had come as any surprise to the man on the middle
cross. In fact, everything was going exactly according to plan. Although His human enemies on earth and His spiritual enemies from
hell were looking on in gleeful triumph at His apparent defeat, Jesus
Christ knew His Father was looking on from heaven in approval as
He fulfilled His appointed destiny.

It had all come to this. He had been born for this . . . lived for
this . . . was now dying for this. This was His mission coming down
to its final moments.

It had been six hours since He'd walked at the vortex of a chaotic
swirling mass of people pressing in on Him; yet it was the most singularly solitary path any man would ever take. His journey led through

the narrow, winding streets of the city, out the main gate, up the ugly hill shaped like a skull and finished with Him nailed to the rough wood of the cross, lifted, suspended between heaven and earth.

Physically, He was more dead than alive. By all rights He should have died during the flesh-shredding flogging He'd received from shoulders to ankles with whips tipped with bone, metal and glass, aptly given the gruesome nickname "cat-o'-nine tails." Many condemned men never made it past the scourging, succumbing to shock and blood loss. That scourging had followed hours of pounding from fists and staffs doing their furious work before the whips did theirs. Eager priests took out their hatred on the one who had threatened their well-ordered and immensely profitable religious system. Roman soldiers released their fiendish pleasure and pent-up anger at this man who represented the troublesome Jewish people at the armpit of their empire.

Jesus was nearly unrecognizable; His face a bloody, puffy pulp with patches of beard missing, His head still crowned by inch-thick thorns, His body a bleeding mass of wounds, welts, lumps and shredded flesh.

For six hours He'd hung on the cross, fastened by rusty spikes driven through wrist and ankle bones. The evil genius of crucifixion was that it forced the condemned man into a position that both sent spasms of screaming pain through every limb and made breathing an immense effort. To gain each breath, He had to coerce His body upward with all His weight on the spike-secured feet. Unable to keep His weight on His feet due to the agonizing pain, He would slide down, rubbing the raw flesh of the open wounds on His back on the splintered wood and bringing all weight now onto His wrists. Excruciating spasms of pain from the fingertips into the chest, coupled with the need to breathe, would compel Him back up on His feet for another breath. The horrific process was repeated over and over until the combination of exhaustion, blood loss and asphyxiation brought expiration. Six hours on the cross preceded by the hours of beating now made each breath a supreme act of the will more than an effort of physical strength.

He'd been emotionally battered as much as He had been beaten physically. Taunts, curses, jeers, blasphemies and vile words were spewed on Him like demonic vomit splattered all over His soul by the very people He'd come to save. Only the tears and soft words of love spoken by His mother and a handful of His other followers had softened the onslaught. It seemed that all sinful humanity's hatred, spanning all of history, against a holy God that dared to interfere with claims of personal sovereignty was hurled at Him in those hours, amplified by the frenzied demonic cacophony from the realm of the spirit.

As horrific and awful as the physical and emotional abuse was, the spiritual ramifications were far greater. Three hours into His time on the cross, at noon, the sun had suddenly refused to shine, throwing the entire scene into a palpable, eerie darkness. The crowd, vociferous before, was stunned into fearful murmuring. Not long after, Jesus looked up and desperately pleaded with His Father, asking Him why He had deserted Him. For the only time in all eternity, He was completely, utterly alone—isolated in the darkness of iniquity from His Father. The crushing weight of humanity's sin was laid on Him, separating Him from His Father and suffocating Him with the immensity of all the innumerable selfish thoughts, attitudes, words and actions produced by every person who had ever lived and would ever live.

The King of heaven was experiencing the reality of hell.

Yet He had borne it all with incredible grace and patience. In all those hours He only spoke a handful of times. Those listening closely recognized that He was quoting and completing Scriptures written hundreds of years before—from Psalms 22 and 69, Isaiah 53 and others.

For six hours He'd fought on so many levels. He was thirsty . . . so thirsty. A soldier gave Him some sour vinegar on a sponge to allow His parched throat some relief. It seemed that He was waiting for something . . .

It was three in the afternoon now, the time of the afternoon sacrifice in the Temple. Every day an innocent lamb was slain on the altar as a substitute for sins—a daily practice of multiple sacrifices that had been going on for centuries. Yet, every sacrifice was incomplete, each one a temporary foreshadowing of the one perfect sacrifice that only the Messiah could make. In the Temple, a priest raised his knife to slash the neck of the lamb.

At *that* moment, Jesus stretched Himself to His full height, lifting His head with a look of victory and shouted to heaven and the rest of the universe, *"Tetelestai!"* "Finished!" His shout echoed across the valley and through all eternity.

Around the cross, below and above the cross, there was instant response to the word spoken in such triumph.

All across the crowd heads snapped up in astonishment. This was not the last gasping utterance of a defeated, condemned man . . . a breath from death. It was a familiar word, a word that meant many things—"Completed! Accomplished! Done! Fulfilled!" The tense made the single word blossom with even more meaning.

"It *is* finished . . . it *stands* finished . . . it will *always* be finished!"

The *soldiers* knew that word—it was a warrior's roar of victory. This was the cry of a combatant shouting His conquest at the end of a battle. They'd stood over their defeated foes many times bellowing that same word! Operation successful, enemy defeated, victory secure . . . we've won! Never had they expected it to come from someone they assumed they'd conquered. This was a dying man declaring His dominion over death itself! They hadn't killed Him; He'd killed death! The centurion, who in growing wonder had watched this unlikely Warrior from His conversation with Pilate to His cry from the cross, looked up in awe and said, "Surely, this man was the Son of God."

Servants instantly recognized the word—it was the word they used to report to their master that their assigned task was completed as ordered. Mission accomplished . . . task completed . . . job done. Some found themselves remembering what they'd heard Jesus say more than once: "The Son of Man did not come to be served, but to serve, and to give his life as ransom for many." The Savior sent to serve had completed His assignment, the greatest act of service done in unconditional love was now accomplished.

Artists, musicians and authors resonated with the word. How many times had they put the finishing touches of color on a painting or put the final period at the end of a sentence or a musical note completing a composition and said with satisfied relief, "Finished!" The infinitely big picture that only God Almighty could see now had its last brushstrokes—a portrait of humanity's salvation He'd been painting from the dawn of eternity—now finished in blood. The exclamation point on the story of salvation He'd been writing across history—His Story—had just been capped with thunderous punctuation. All the salvation stories of history and the specifics of religious rituals now made perfect sense. The melody of salvation's symphony came to a climactic, fulfilling crescendo of completion with that cry from the cross.

Merchants looked up with shocked understanding. They *knew* that word! Every time they completed a sale or finished a business transaction they used it. Debt erased . . . paid in full . . . deal done . . . transaction finalized! In the eternal economy of God, sin was a debt to His holiness that had to be paid or the debtor faced the eternal consequences. Continuous sacrifices and acts of contrition could never pay the obligation due to a just and holy God. But now this *one* sacrifice . . . this *one* payment . . . this *one* sum paid in blood had erased the debt of all humanity for all history. He had paid a debt He did not owe for those in infinite debt who could never pay.

Priests and religious leaders found themselves in open-mouthed amazement. This was the word they used to confirm that a sacrificial lamb was faultless and able to be sacrificed—it was perfect . . . spotless . . . completely worthy. It was also the word they used when that sacrifice was completed to signal that sin's penalty had been overcome and its power overruled. Right before their eyes they'd seen the perfect fulfillment of every prophecy from Scripture they'd ever read and every ritual ever performed. No more rituals required. No more innocent blood spilled. No more sacrifices needed. With this sacrifice they were all done. The Lamb of God had taken away the sins of the world. The chief priest and his inner circle, who had stood viciously jeering at Jesus to come down off the cross and save Himself, now realized in shock that He had stayed on the cross to save *them*.

In the Temple, two unseen, omnipotent hands took the fist-thick curtain separating humble worshipers from the Holy of Holies and tore it from top to bottom, forever signaling that the way to a relationship with God was now open—unholy men and women could come, receive forgiveness and live close to the heart of a holy God with hearts now cleansed and changed to become like His.

With that word spoken from the cross, the earth convulsed, as if shaking off the curse it was living under. The rolling shudder of creation cracked streets, streams and stones. Saints, once dead, left their stony confinement, now living and breathing and worshiping in astounded wonder.

In hell, the word sent shock waves throughout the kingdom of darkness. Satan's scheme to usurp God's rule of the universe was shattered. His power to deceive and dominate was devastated. His plan to bring down God's Son so that he would ascend to the throne of light had completely backfired in his face, forever condemning him and his demons to impotent lower regions of outer darkness and fire. The prisoners he claimed as his spoil were now liberated, able to be rescued by repentant faith in the regal ransom of the reigning King of the Universe.

Angels erupted with applause. They could not fully understand the scope of what they'd just witnessed, but they knew this was the apex of Almighty God's plan to restore His relationship with those created in His image.

The Father, hearing His Son speak that word, nodded in somber affirmation. His greatest gift was offered. His greatest act of love was now complete. The seed planted in Bethlehem had come to fruition at Golgotha. The temporary blockage between Father and Son was now removed, their perfect fellowship restored forever. The way to God was now open to everyone, everywhere, who chose to come in humble faith.

Laying His head back on the cross as a weary man lays his head on a pillow at the end of a long day, Jesus rested from His work. He'd completed His course, accomplished His mission. Sin, death and hell were conquered. What He'd done for us could never be duplicated. It doesn't need to be. What needed to be done to bring us back to the heart of God was now fulfilled. Salvation would never be a result of what any of us can do—but always a response in faith to what Jesus has already done.

It was just as the Godhead had planned. One word summed it up and said it all. "It is finished . . . it stands finished . . . it will always be finished!"

Finished!

BEYOND THE STORY
To Help You Think, Pray, Share and Do

1. Which of the word pictures around "finished" resonated with you the most? Why?

2. As you think about what happened in the natural realm at the cross, how does that make you think about how God speaks through nature today?

3. Jesus' shout of victory is the foundation of confident faith for us today. How confident is your faith? How does the story you just read help confident faith to grow in you?

4. What issues in your life do you need to have Jesus apply His finished work on the cross for you? Why not take them to Him now?

7

"Into Your Hands"

"Father, into your hands I commit my spirit."
LUKE 23:46, *NIV*

The oppressive darkness had smothered Golgotha for three hours. It had fallen at noon, when the sun was at its strongest. Suddenly the sun shuddered and refused to shine. For the assembled crowd and the two criminals on either side of Jesus, the darkness was eerie. It was thick and palpable, with a frightening supernatural quality that hushed the jeering mob into uneasy murmurs.

For the man on the middle cross, the darkness represented far more. Even in the midst of His immense suffering, He was conscious of unseen things in the spiritual realm. When the darkness first descended, Jesus realized that even creation could not bear the sight of its Creator hanging between heaven and hell. Later, the darkness buzzed with swarming demonic voices eager to add their taunting blasphemy, beating on Him with fiendish enjoyment.

The darkness abruptly took on an entirely different tone. All other aspects of the darkness—the mockery of the crowd, the apathy of the soldiers, the agony of physical pain, blasphemy from the demonic—had been bearable because He knew He was not alone. Then, suddenly, He felt totally alone. For the first and only time in all eternity the Father, Son and Spirit felt separated, and His desperate cry asking God why He had forsaken Him spoke of His anguish and alienation. His Father had abandoned Him. The silence of separation was deafening.

Jesus knew the answer to His agonizing question. God the Father made His Son, who knew no sin, to become sin on behalf of all humanity. The weight of human iniquity cascaded on Him in wave after wave of every offensive transgression ever committed and every sin that would ever be committed, piling on Him, suffocating Him.

No longer was He just bearing the pain of the cross. The words of Isaiah were being fulfilled:

"He was wounded for our transgressions, He was bruised for our iniquities; the chastisement for our peace was upon Him, and by His stripes we are healed."

Suddenly, it was over. Piercing the sin-induced blackness, supernatural light broke through, first to Jesus as the Father smiled; then creation smiled back and the sun resumed shining its light.

Jesus threw back His head in triumph. His mission was over, His task complete. He shouted with the cry of a victor, the word ringing across the valley and all eternity, "Finished!"

There was just one last thing to do. Laying His head back on the cross as if relaxing into His Father's arms, He said, *"Father, into Your hands I commit My Spirit."* And with that, Jesus released His spirit to His Father.

Every Jewish person instantly recognized His last words that startled everyone who heard it. Jesus had quoted Psalm 31:5. It was the bedtime prayer mothers taught their children to say before they went to sleep every night, telling their heavenly Father they were trusting Him with their spirit through the night while they slept. It was the prayer Mary had taught Jesus as a boy. Jesus had quoted that verse and prayed that prayer, but He had added one word—"Father."

That one word said so much; the relationship between Father and Son had been restored. The sense of separation was ended. The alienation caused by the load of sin had been overcome by the love of the Son. The punishment was over . . . Paradise awaited. Sin, Satan and eternal separation in hell were conquered . . . and death, the last enemy, was defeated. Even as He released His spirit, Jesus had been in control to the end. He had died confidently, willingly, victoriously.

"Father, into Your hands I commit my Spirit." In those words, Jesus taught us how to die. Death is not an enemy to be feared but a doorway through which we follow our Savior in eternal fellowship with Him. Death may mark the end of our earthly physical existence, but our spirit lives on eternally. If we know Jesus as Savior, we can willingly release our spirit into the Father's hands. We can fall asleep in our Father's arms with confidence and peace.

Even as Jesus released His spirit to the Father, the Father simultaneously released signs that signaled the salvation His Son had just secured.

Light rolled back the darkness as the sun shone again. Three hours of sin-provoked darkness ended as salvation light permeated the scene. Jesus had said that men don't come to the Father because they love darkness more than light. Sin and darkness go together; not only does darkness try to hide sin, but it also obscures our view of who God really is. The oppressive darkness that had ruled for three hours at Calvary was now overcome with salvation brilliance. To see Jesus on the cross is to see the holiness and love of God perfectly revealed. Because of the cross, faith is not a leap in the dark; it is a step into the light. Walking with Jesus means overcoming darkness in every form.

The veil in the Temple, separating unholy people from the presence of a holy God, was torn down the middle. That veil, a fist thick, 30 feet high and 60 feet long, protected the Holy of Holies. The Temple was segmented and segregated, allowing people to approach God from a prescribed distance. The farthest away from the Holy of Holies were the Gentiles. Then came Jewish women. Next were Jewish men, Jewish priests and finally, the High Priest, who could only enter the Holy of Holies once a year to offer a sacrifice of blood on behalf of unholy people. Sovereignly strong "hands" took the veil that represented separation between God and man and ripped it in half from top to bottom. Suddenly the way to a relationship with a holy God was open to everyone no matter his or her race, color, creed, language, and no matter how horrible the sin. With His one sacrifice, the blood of Jesus makes a relationship with our heavenly Father a reality if we will come in repentance and faith.

An earthquake showed creation rejoicing as Jesus rescued it from sin's curse. Ever since the garden of Eden, when sin entered a world that God had created in perfection, creation had groaned under the curse of sin. Sickness, storms and savagery—all are symptoms of the curse. Jesus' victory on the cross rescued creation from the curse of sin. Someday our sovereign God will completely remake creation, and even now we live in days when He intervenes in healing, deliverance and protection from sin's attack.

Graves opened across Jerusalem and saints stepped out of their tombs, responding to a supernatural summons in resurrection wonder. Their Savior would rise from the dead on Sunday morning; but on this Friday marked by death they were modeling the power of God to overcome the grave. Later the apostle Paul would revel, "Death is swallowed up in victory. O death, where is your victory? O death, where is your sting? For sin is the sting that results in death, and the law gives sin its power. How we thank God, who gives us victory over sin and death through Jesus Christ our Lord!" From that time on, physical death has released us from a physical body that isn't meant to live forever. Instead, we trade it in for a glorified resurrection body reunited with our spirit that lives in supernatural splendor in the presence of our Savior.

A hardened Centurion was redeemed as he watched the Son of God die for him. The bodies and hearts of Roman soldiers were covered by steel. They were famous for their callous disregard for any religion but the power of their swords. Yet, this man whom tradition has named Longinus, found his hardened heart humbled and broken by the regal power of a King far greater than his emperor. He had watched Jesus face impossible human opposition and horrible physical oppression with dignity, grace and courage. He'd watched the man of the middle cross forgive the very ones who'd put Him there, including the centurion himself. He watched Jesus die in triumph and realized the man on the middle cross was more than just a man; Jesus was the Son of God. He'd watched Jesus face it all as a far braver warrior than he could ever be. He yielded his allegiance to a new Master and Savior and was the first Gentile to be redeemed because of the cross.

Many who gathered around the cross missed the supernatural signals from the Father that day. The crowd went home in sorrow. The disciples fled and hid in fear. All the soldiers but one went into Jerusalem to drown the day's events in strong drink. Religious leaders took refuge behind Temple walls, feeling puzzled and perplexed about the words of Jesus and the torn Temple veil.

Sunday would change everything.

Today we look back on a day we can now call "Good Friday" because we understand the seven last words of Jesus from the cross. They humble us with their love and grace. They amaze us as we understand to whom they were spoken. They draw us to repent again and put our faith in Jesus the Christ in fresh surrender. They comfort us as we realize that even death has been defeated by our wonderful Savior. And when our time on earth is done, we can rest in our Father's arms and say with grateful confidence, as Jesus did, "Father, into Your hands I commit my spirit."

BEYOND THE STORY
To Help You Think, Pray, Share and Do

1. "Now I lay me down to sleep . . ." Bedtime prayers with children are universal. Some of Jesus' last words from the cross were part of a common bedtime prayer in His land. If you have children, how are you helping them learn how to pray? In what ways are your family being intentional about building faith into your children?

2. It's been said that what's going on in the spiritual realm also happens visibly in the natural realm. When Jesus yielded His spirit into His father's hands, spiritual realities had natural manifestations. What do those natural events tell you about what was going on in the spiritual realm?

3. You've read many stories about the day that changed forever—told through the eyes of many different people with many different responses to what Jesus did for us. Which stories meant the most to you? Why? What choices are you making because of what you've experienced through these stories?

4. How can you live out your thanks to the Lord for what He's done for you? Who can you bring to the cross to meet Him . . . so He can change their forever, too?

SCRIPTURE REFERENCES

Page 20: "Who do people say that I am?" Luke 9:18-27.

Page 22: *"Anyone who intends to come with me . . ."* Matthew 16:24,26.

Page 23: *"If you're embarrassed over me . . ."* Mark 8:38.

Page 25: "You . . . will be the true liberator . . ." Luke 9:28-34.

Page 26: *"This is My Son, whom I love . . ."* Luke 9:35.

Page 29: "Behold . . . the Lamb of God . . ." John 1:29.

Page 29: "Come and see." John 1:39.

Page 30: "Follow Me." John 1:43.

Page 33: "Men . . . tomorrow, I am going to Jerusalem . . ." Luke 9:21-25.

Page 34: "Do you know what those miserable Samaritans said to us?" Luke 9:51-54.

Page 35: *"You do not know what kind of spirit you are of . . ."* Luke 9:56.

Page 37: "Get behind me, Satan." Matthew 16:23.

Page 38: "The Lord has need of it." Matthew 21:2-3.

Page 39: "Oh, Jerusalem, Jerusalem . . ." Matthew 23:37-38.

Page 39: "Tell the daughter of Zion . . ." Matthew 21:5.

Page 40: "Hosanna to the Son of David . . ." Matthew 21:9.

Page 41: "Stop this!" Luke 19:39.

Page 41: "If I told these people to be quiet . . ." Luke 19:40.

Page 46: *"I will bring you out . . ."* Exodus 6:6.

Page 46: *"I will rescue you . . ."* Exodus 6:6.

Page 47: *"I will redeem you . . ."* Exodus 6:6.

Page 47: *"I will take you . . ."* Exodus 6:7.

Page 47: "I have deeply desired to eat . . ." Luke 22:15-16.

Page 48: "Lord, You're not going to wash my feet . . ." John 13:6.

Page 48: "Peter, you don't understand . . ." John 13:7.

Page 48: "No! You'll never wash my feet . . ." John 13:8.

Page 48: "Then, please," he said meekly . . ." John 13:9.

Page 49: "Do you understand what I've done for you . . ." John 13:12-23.

Page 51: "The highest needs to become the lowest . . ." Mark 10:31.

Page 51: "I have chosen to be your servant . . ." Matthew 20:28.

Page 52: *"But He was pierced for our transgressions . . ."* Isaiah 53:5.

Page 63: "This is My Father's house . . ." Mark 11:17.

Page 65: "What will you give me . . ." Matthew 26:15.

Page 66: "One of you is going to betray me." Matthew 26:21.

Page 66: "Surely not I, Rabbi?" Matthew 26:25.

Page 67: "Do what you're going to do . . ." John 13:27.

Page 68: "Remember, the one I greet . . . " Matthew 26:48.

Page 68: "Friend, do what you've come for." Matthew 26:50.

Page 68: "Greetings, Rabbi!" Matthew 26:49.

Page 68: "Judas . . . You betray the Son of Man with a kiss?" Luke 22:48.

Page 68: "Who is it you are looking for?" John 18:4-8.

Page 70: *"Even my friend in whom I trusted . . ."* Psalm 41:9.

Page 70: "I have sinned." Matthew 27:4.

Page 71: *"Give me my wages . . ."* Zechariah 11:12-13.

Page 76: "This Jesus is unlike anyone I've ever seen or heard about." Matthew 27:19.

Page 79: "What charges are you bringing against this man?" John 18:29-31.

Page 79: "Are you King of the Jews?" John 18:33-38.

Page 81: "We have a law..." John 19:7.
Page 83: "I will have him flogged..." Luke 23:16.
Page 83: "Crucify.....crucify...crucify..." Luke 23:21.
Page 83: "Where do you come from?" John 19:9.
Page 83: "I came into the world, to testify to the truth." John 18:37.
Page 84: "What is truth?" John 18:38.
Page 84: "I find no basis for a charge..." John 18:38-39.
Page 84: "Have nothing to do with this..." Matthew 27:19.
Page 85: "Give us Barabbas." Matthew 27:21-22.
Page 85: "Do you refuse to speak to me?" John 19:10.
Page 85: "You have no power over me..." John 19:11.
Page 85: "Do you want me to crucify your king?" John 19:15.
Page 86: "I find nothing wrong with this man." Matthew 27:24.
Page 89: "Barabbas, you have been sentenced to die..." John 18:39.
Page 91: "I have found this man, Christ, innocent of all wrongdoing." Luke 23:16.
Page 91: "NO! Crucify him!" John 18:40.
Page 91: "Would you have me crucify your king?" John 19:15.
Page 91: "All right, which one do you want me to release to you..." Matthew 27:17.
Page 104: "It is written... My house shall be called a house of prayer..." Mark 11:17.
Page 107: "Who are you?" John 18:19.
Page 107: "How dare you speak to the High Priest like that?" John 18:22.
Page 107: "If I've said something wrong, prove it." John 18:23.
Page 107: "Aren't you going to answer any of these charges?" Matthew 26:62.
Page 109: "I adjure you by the living God..." Matthew 26:63.
Page 109: "Tell us... are You the Messiah..." Matthew 26:63.
Page 110: "I AM!... and you will see the Son of Man..." Mark 14:62.
Page 110: "Blasphemy! He has claimed to be God!" Mark 14:64.
Page 111: "Death... death to the blasphemer!" Matthew 26:66.
Page 115: "And when the centurion... heard his cry..." Mark 15:39.
Page 117: "He had claimed to be equal with God—to be God's own Son." Matthew 25:65-66.
Page 119: "Father, forgive them..." Luke 23:34.
Page 119: "This very day you shall be with me in Paradise." Luke 23:43.
Page 119: "TETELESTAI! IT IS FINISHED!" Luke 23:46.
Page 119: "Surely this man was the Son of God!" Mark 15:39.
Page 123: "How do you do the things you're doing..." John 3:2.
Page 123: "Just as Moses lifted up the snake..." John 3:14-15.
Page 124: "*But, oh, how few believe it...*" Isaiah 53:1.
Page 124: "*See, my servant will act wisely...*" Isaiah 52:13-15.
Page 124: "Are you the Messiah, the Son of the Blessed One?" Mark 14:61.
Page 124: "I AM!" Mark 14:62.
Page 125: "*He was despised and rejected by men...*" Isaiah 53:3.
Page 126: "*He was oppressed and afflicted...*" Isaiah 53:7.
Page 126: "Father, forgive them..." Luke 23:34.
Page 126: "*We all, like sheep, have gone astray...*" Isaiah 53:6.
Page 127: "*Yet it was the LORD's will to crush him...*" Isaiah 53:10.
Page 127: "My God, my God, why have you forsaken me?" Mark 15:34.
Page 127: "*But he was pierced for our transgressions...*" Isaiah 53:5.
Page 129: "Father, forgive them..." Luke 23:34.
Page 132: "Please forgive me, please forgive me..." Luke 7:38.
Page 133: "Simon... I have something to tell you." Luke 7:40-43.

Page 133: "Do you see this woman?" Luke 7:44-47.
Page 133: "Your sins are forgiven . . ." Luke 7:48-50.
Page 134: "It is finished!" Luke 23:46.
Page 139: "I AM . . ." John 18:5.
Page 141: "Father, forgive them . . ." Luke 23:34.
Page 142: "Dear woman . . . here is your son." John 19:26-27.
Page 146: "But you . . . who do *you* say I am?" Matthew 16:15.
Page 146: "You are the Messiah, the Sone of the Living God!" Matthew 16:16.
Page 147: "No, Lord! This will never happen to You." Matthew 16:22.
Page 147: "Get behind me, Satan!" Matthew 16:23.
Page 147: "This is My beloved Son." Matthew 17:5.
Page 148: "It's not me, is it, Lord?" Mark 14:19.
Page 148: "Even if everyone runs away, I never will!" Matthew 26:33.
Page 148: "Simon . . . Simon . . . Satan has asked me if he can have you . . ." Luke 22:31-32.
Page 148: "Lord, I'm ready to go to prison for You." Luke 22:33.
Page 148: "Before the rooster crows twice this night . . ." Mark 14:30.
Page 149: "Why are you sleeping . . ." Mark 14:37.
Page 149: "I know . . . the spirit is willing but the flesh is weak." Mark 14:38.
Page 149: "It's time. Get up . . . my betrayer is coming." Matthew 26:46.
Page 150: "Put your sword away!" Matthew 26:52-54.
Page 150: "Weren't you with the Galilean too?" Matthew 26:69-74.
Page 154: "Finished!" Luke 23:46.
Page 162: "Nevertheless, not My will but Yours be done." Luke 22:42.
Page 163: "This must happen so the Scripture might be fulfilled . . ." Matthew 26:54.
Page 163: "*Eloi, Eloi, lama sabachthani* . . ." Mark 15:34.
Page 164: "It is finished!" Luke 23:46.
Page 164: "Father, into Your hands I commit My spirit . . ." Luke 23:46.
Page 170: "*Father, forgive them* . . ." Luke 23:34.
Page 171: "Are you the Messiah, the Son of God?" Mark 14:61.
Page 176: "*He poured out his life unto to death* . . ." Isaiah 53:12.
Page 177: "Father, forgive them . . ." Luke 23:34.
Page 182: "Aren't you the Christ?" Luke 23:39.
Page 183: "Don't you even fear God when you are dying?" Luke 23:40-41.
Page 183: "Jesus, remember me . . ." Luke 23:42.
Page 183: "I tell you the truth, this very day . . ." Luke 23:43.
Page 184: "Today you will be with me in Paradise." Luke 23:43.
Page 190: "*Eloi, Eloi! Lama sabachthani?*" Mark 15:34.
Page 190: "He's calling for Elijah . . ." Matthew 27:47.
Page 190: "Yes . . . let's see if Elijah comes to save him." Matthew 27:49.
Page 190: "*My God, my God, why have you forsaken me?*" Psalm 22:1-2,8,11-18.
Page 194: "*And a sword will pierce your own soul too.*" Luke 2:35.
Page 197: "*Woman . . . behold your Son.*" John 19:26-27.
Page 200: "*I thirst.*" John 19:28.
Page 200: "*Save me, O God, for the floodwaters are up to my neck.*" Psalm 69:1-4,7-9,13-21.
Page 211: "*Tetelestai!*" Luke 23:46.
Page 211: "Surely, this man was the Son of God." Mark 15:39.
Page 211: "The Son of Man did not come to be served . . ." Matthew 20:28.
Page 216: "*He was wounded for our transgressions* . . ." Isaiah 53:5.
Page 216: "*Father, into Your hands I commit My Spirit.*" Luke 23:46.
Page 218: "Death is swallowed up in victory . . ." 1 Corinthians 15:54-57.

CRM EMPOWERING LEADERS

CRM (Church Resource Ministries) is a movement committed to developing leaders to strengthen and multiply the Church worldwide.

More than 350 CRM missionaries live and minister in nations on every continent, coaching, mentoring and apprenticing those called to lead the Christian movement in their settings. This results in the multiplication of godly leaders who have a passion for their work and who are empowered to multiply their lives and ministry. Through them, CRM stimulates movements of fresh, authentic churches, holistic in nature, so that the name of God is renowned among the nations.

For more information, visit **www.crmleaders.org**.